# The Mandala Kitchen

# The Mandala Kitchen

## 100 recipes to heal and restore your gut

Marlien Wright

JACANA

*For my beautiful daughters Milla & Ava, the two most delightful hungry hooligans I know, thank you for letting me to see this adventure called life through your eyes; and for D – no day passes without us feeling the emptiness where you used to be.*

## Acknowledgements

In the spirit of collaboration and bravery I have hooked up with sexy ceramists *Rialheim*. Thank you Rialheim for inspiring me to be brave and letting me use your sublime ceramics in most of the food images in this book. If you would like to purchase some Rialheim ceramic happiness, visit www.rialheim.co.za.

A heartfelt thank you to my friend and talented photographer, Peter Maddock Wilkins, who generously supplied all the lovely lifestyle pictures in this book. Thank you for persuading me continuously out of my comfort zone, Peter. Stay in touch with Peter's photography via Instagram: @petermaddockwilkins.

A huge thank you to Spirit Café & Spirit Yoga Studio and owner Kate Ball for keeping me bendy, and allowing me to use some of the delicious and gut-loving recipes that are served at Spirit Café. For more information on where you can find a Spirit Café or attend a Spirit Yoga class or retreat, visit www.spiritcafe.co.za.

Thank you to the Wellness Warehouse Café for sharing three of their fabulously healthy recipes for this book, and thank goodness for the Wellness Warehouse for stocking all the ingredients I love to use and for continuing to blaze new health trails everywhere. To buy all your favourite healthy ingredients online, visit www.wellnesswarehouse.com.

A special thank you to Justin and Erica Sonnenburg, whose book *The Good Gut* has been hugely inspirational in my gut-health journey, as well as for allowing me to share some of their delicious gut-healthy recipes here.

A big thank you to Marrow for allowing me to share two of their yummy and nutritious broth recipes here. Marrow is Cape Town's very first bone broth bar: https://www.marrowbroth.co.za/.

First published by Jacana Media (Pty) Ltd in 2018

10 Orange Street
Sunnyside
Auckland Park 2092
South Africa
+2711 628 3200
www.jacana.co.za

© Marlien Wright, 2018

All rights reserved.

ISBN 978-1-4314-2688-1

Design by Shawn Paikin and Maggie Davey
Food photography by Marlien Wright
Lifestyle photography by Peter Maddock Wilkins
Editing by Megan Mance
Proofreading by Lara Jacob
Index by Megan Mance
Set in Bodoni Egyptian Pro & Bodoni Classic Chancery
Printed and bound by Imago
Job no. 003300

See a complete list of Jacana titles at www.jacana.co.za

# Contents

## SENSIBLE SWEETS

## FUSSY OFFSPRING

## MUNCHIES FOR YOUR MICROBES

# Introduction

# Introduction

## The Mandala Kitchen

Inside all of us, there is an inherent healthy and happy state that we have the power to unlock. I believe that once you have experienced this state of harmony and unity, an intense yearning to return to it awakens.

We are made up of water, tissue, a little stardust and, as it turns out, a large community of microbes (bacteria). In ongoing scientific research, it has come to light that our microbes can play an essential role in our wellbeing.

Our bodies are a host to a community of symbiotic microbes that has evolved over thousands of years to serve us, performing essential functions in the body. Their agenda is simple – the healthier the host the greater the longevity for their home.

By acknowledging the importance of our microbe community in relation to our best health, we can unify and approach our wellbeing from a new perspective. This book is meant to serve as a guide along this journey, to provide delicious recipes to feed your microbes with the ingredients that will promote their ability to multiply and diversify.

In this book I refer to the microbe community using a variety of terminology – gut bugs, good bacteria, microbiome or microbiota. They all refer to microbes.

## Gut feelings

The topic of gut health is often discussed in the media, various books have been published on the subject and there is ongoing research on how our gut health can be linked to our overall good health (and on the flip side, many diseases). Could it be that optimal health, our moods and our ability to fight disease resides in our gut? In fact, our gut is often referred to as our 'second brain'.

But which foods and lifestyle practices promotes optimal gut health? Terminology such as the microbiome or microbiota may be unfamiliar to you, but they simply refer to the community of internal 'bugs' or good bacteria in your digestive system, and more specifically in the large intestine. Our digestive tracts are populated by symbiotic bacteria that regulate, affect and assist with every single body function we have. Microbes are responsible for:

- Converting sugars to short-chain fatty acids for energy
- Crowding out pathogens (bad bacteria)
- Digesting food

- Helping our body absorb nutrients such as calcium and iron
- Keeping our Ph. balanced
- Maintaining the integrity of the gut lining
- Metabolising drugs
- Modulating genes
- Neutralising cancer-causing compounds
- Producing digestive enzymes
- Synthesising B-complex vitamins
- Synthesising fat-soluble vitamins
- Synthesising hormones
- Training the immune system to distinguish friend from foe

Below I dive a little more deeply into how our immunity, risk of inflammation, mood and weight management can be influenced by our gut health.

## Immunity

In our modern society where cancer, digestive and auto-immune disease are rife, science is discovering the connection between gut health and a strong or weak immune system. Our microbes are in charge of the correct gene expression, which means our microbes can switch gene expression on or off, and have the ability to crowd out the bad guys, making our gut health the most essential component in a strong immune system that wages war against disease, not against our own bodies.

Researchers' findings suggest that 70% of the immune system lives in the gut and gut bacteria assist your immune system's T cells to develop – teaching them the difference between a foreign substance and the body's own tissues. This is an extremely important process that determines what your immune system responds to and how, and the success of this critical process is determined, in part, by the health of your gut. When there's a mistake in the process, for instance if there is an overgrowth of one specific type of bacteria, it can lead your body's immune system to begin waging war on your own cells, the hallmark of auto-immune disorders.

Researchers discover new information almost daily in regard to which microbes promotes the best gut health, but from what has been discovered so far it seems essential that your gut microbe community be as diverse as possible and that no one microbe overcrowds the rest.

## Inflammation & leaky gut syndrome

In addition to regulating immune responses, research also suggests that microbes regulate which particles pass through the intestinal lining into the rest of the body. Healthy digestive tracts are designed with small gates that allow digested foods to pass while keeping out larger food particles and other antigens (foreign particles that cause immune reactions). However, in a leaky gut, the gates in the intestinal lining gets damaged by a western diet rich in refined and gluten-rich foods; once the gut's lining has been compromised with these perforations, it allows large food particles and unwanted substances to enter the rest of the body. Once inside, they are rightly treated as foreign invaders and cause immune reactions that trigger inflammation, which in turn triggers disease.

With its role in training your immune system and acting as a gatekeeper to the rest of your body, the gut is arguably the centre of your health. For those with arthritis and other auto-immune conditions whose symptoms are exacerbated or created by poor gut health, healing the gut can reverse their conditions. For everyone else, healing the gut makes developing an auto-immune condition, food sensitivity and/or inflammation less likely.

## Weight management

We have always known that there's a communication pathway from the gut to the brain, but what science has discovered recently is that messages from the gut to the brain don't simply say 'feed me'; messages from the gut also tell our brain which foods to choose. In other words, by restoring your gut health, your cravings can be controlled and changed from unhealthy to healthy foods, promote feelings of satiety and also extract fewer calories from food.

## Mood

Ongoing studies indicate there could be a link between intestinal dysfunction, depression, anxiety and sleep disorders. Serotonin is a neurotransmitter; it is responsible for regulating mood, appetite and sleep. The right amount of serotonin in the brain produces a relaxed and positive outlook. As it turns out, approximately 90% of the serotonin in the body is located in the gut. Can we treat depression, anxiety and behavioural problems by normalising the bacteria in the bowels? Perhaps by addressing gut health you can also move from chronic low mood to chronic good mood.

# Knowledge is power

During my research on gut health I read wonderful books such as *The Microbiome Solution* by MD Robynne Chutkan and *The Mind Gut Connection* by Emeran Mayer, as well as various articles that have been published on the subject. I found the research and delicious recipes in Justin and Erica's Sonnenburg's book *The Good Gut* especially helpful. With their permission, I have included some of them here. They are all marked with 'The Good

Gut' in their titles. Thank you Erica and Justin for allowing me to share them!

For most of us, it's the prebiotics in the food we eat that has the greatest effect on the health of our gut and the bacteria in it. A food may be good or bad for you because of its ability to change the populations of bacteria and the chemicals they produce in either a positive or negative way. A detailed explanation of which foods promote thriving gut health is provided in the chapter called Remove, Replace & Restore.

In conclusion, unlike our genes, we can change our microbiome to improve our health at any time during our lives; it literally is never too late. For an optimally functioning microbiome it has led me to the belief that what we eat (or exclude) ultimately has the best (or worst) effect on our overall (gut) health. It has inspired me to specifically collect and develop recipes that assist in healing the gut and providing the food for your good bugs to thrive, multiply and diversify. As in my first book, *The Yoga Kitchen: 100 Easy Superfood Recipes*, I have endeavoured to make the recipes simple, time saving and family friendly.

To make the journey to embark on good gut health easier, I have also included:

- The Gentle Start Suggestions chapter to be used as a guideline on how to start your journey
- Meal ideas for lunchboxes in the chapter called Lunchbox Love to keep your gut happy on the go
- Child-friendly meals in the chapter titled Fussy Offspring that have been fool-proof with my two girls
- I have also selected and included some fabulous recipes from *The Good Gut*, and a few of my favourites from Wellness (Warehouse) Café, Spirit Café and Marrow for gut-healthy food choices on the go.


For more information on how to start your gut-healing journey, read the next chapter titled Remove, Replace & Restore.

Remove,
Replace
& Restore

# Remove, Replace & Restore

When we start investigating why our gut health may be in trouble, especially so in western society, the following has to be taken into consideration. We have universally included chlorine in our public drinking water and instituted pasteurisation, gassing, radiation and the addition of various other chemicals to stop bacteria growth in our food products to increase shelf life. The steps we take to eliminate pathogens in our food also happen to destroy beneficial bacteria.

Diseases such as IBS, auto-immune disease, Crohn's disease and Celiac disease are becoming more and more common, especially in countries following a western diet lacking a wide variety of plant-based wholefoods. The lethal combination of not nearly enough fibre (prebiotics) and a diet high in undesirable ingredients such as refined flours/gluten, sugar, preservatives, nasty additives, trans-fats and GMO ingredients and, last but not least, second-hand antibiotics are causing havoc with our digestive health. You may be unaware that your gut health is less than good, so below I have compiled a list of signs and symptoms that can be indicators of an unhealthy gut:

- low energy
- bloating
- abdominal pain
- constipation or diarrhoea
- brain fog and low mood
- auto-immune disorder
- frequent infections
- food intolerance and skin disorders
- joint pain
- inflammation

If you are suffering from any of these symptoms then your plan of action is a simple three-step process – remove, replace and restore.

# Remove

**Remove** harmful medications, foods and lifestyle practices that are damaging your microbiome. This will initially be very difficult, and you will find that you are often reverting to old habits. But the best piece of advice I can offer you is from the cheeky mouth of my 8-year-old daughter: 'just chillax mom'. In adult-speak this translates as 'give yourself a break', simply put it behind you and start again.

## Foods and lifestyle choices

- Refined flours, gluten and sugar
  Refined flour foods (even the gluten-free varieties) lack the fibre that our microbes need to thrive. In addition, any refined flour gets absorbed in the small intestine, never reaching the large intestine where the real gut-health magic happens. Refined flour also turns into sugar as soon as it is absorbed, spiking your insulin levels, and lacks any real nutrition.

  Sugar feeds gut bacteria, but not the good bacteria. It's therefore essential to eliminate sugar almost entirely, apart from the occasional well-deserved treat, or allowing a teaspoon of sugar here and there to reduce acidity in a recipe. I have, however, included some gut-friendly recipes to satisfy your sweet tooth in this book. Enjoying the occasional treat is good for the soul, and when chosen well can also be nourishing for our bodies.

- Antibiotics, growth hormones and other lifestyle choices to avoid
  Avoid antibiotics when possible. Antibiotics are a wonderful medical invention and have saved many lives, but are often used unnecessarily. Have an honest discussion with your medical practitioner about what the outcome will be when not using antibiotics – should that outcome be a couple more days of bed rest I am sure you can come to the right conclusion as to whether to use them or not. When antibiotic treatment is unavoidable ask your medical practitioner to consider prescribing a single-strain antibiotic rather than a wide spectrum antibiotic (single strains can be less damaging to your good microbe community).

- Dairy
  Choose *A2 origin dairy products, and preferably cultured such as yoghurt, kefir or aged cheeses.

  The lactose in milk is hard to digest for the human body; it is after all designed for a baby cow with an entirely different constitution to a human, and becomes even more difficult to digest once it has been pasteurised (or even worse, super pasteurised) as the heating of milk during the pasteurisation process makes lactose almost impossible to digest and destroys the enzymes that would have assisted the digestion process. There are two solutions to keep dairy in your diet: Source a reputable supplier of raw, unpasteurised milk or stick to cultured dairy only.

  Consider choosing only cultured (albeit being pasteurised) dairy products, which have the added benefit of being a good source of probiotics (good bacteria) and which will assist your body to digest the lactose.

*\* A2 milk comes from jersey cows, Asian and African breeds). Friesen and Holstein dairy cows (the black and white kind) produce a small but significant amount of beta casein A1. Epidemiological studies have implicated the consumption of A1 in the development of heart disease, type 1 diabetes, autism and schizophrenia.*

- GMO, unfermented soy

  Soy can be consumed in small amounts if it's organic (non GMO) and fermented (cultured). Consuming large amounts of GMO soy can increase your oestrogen levels, which have been linked to breast cancer (among others).

- Sweeteners

  Artificial sweeteners like aspartame, saccharin and sucralose have a direct effect on gut health for the worse. New research indicates that artificial sweeteners can boost sugar intolerance as a marker of diabetes and may increase gut microbes linked to obesity and metabolic disease.

- Anti-bacterial products

  Avoid anti-bacterial products' rather using ordinary soap in a less aggressive approach to staying clean. Allow kids to get dirty because their exposure to the microbes in soil plays a very important role in cultivating a thriving gut garden of their own, thus also promoting diversity in their microbe community.

- Pesticides

  Grow your own vegetables, or purchase them from a reputable organic grocer/market with local, seasonal produce. Pesticides and GMO foods are not positive contributors in your quest for thriving gut health, so avoid them whenever possible. Often during nutrition workshops I get asked by participants what the best course of action is if they can't find, or afford, organic produce. The simple answer is that for your optimal health you need to consume an abundance and wide variety vegetables. Organic versus non-organic fruits and vegetables is a matter of weighing up two evils and deciding which is less damaging. Pesticides are not ideal, but vegetable consumption – and lots of it – is essential for your best health. So wash, scrub and peel veggies if they are of a non-organic origin, but do eat them!

- Chlorine

  Consider investing in a water purifier to remove chlorine from drinking water. Install a water-saving tank for showers and baths which will be filled with rain water sans chlorine.

# Replace

**Replace** good bacteria. Include plenty of fermented foods that are rich in good bacteria.

Fermenting or culturing food simply refers to an old-fashioned preserving method that has been used to increase the shelf life of the food. Fermented foods like sauerkraut, kombucha, kefir, kimchi, unpasteurised miso paste and yoghurt are all good sources of probiotics. When including these foods daily, it will assist in re-seeding your gut garden by introducing a wider spectrum of bacteria to the gut. I have included some recipes in the chapter Crunch

& Cultured to empower you to start culturing at home, but should you wish to purchase fermented foods to keep life simple they are easy to find in the fridge at your local health-food stores and even some supermarkets.

# Restore

**Restore** your microbiome with foods that will enable your gut health to flourish. This is really where the healing starts! Fibre, fibre, fibre! We need to eat a more plant-based diet. The fibre in plant foods provides the food (prebiotics) for good bacteria to flourish – in fact the whole fruit and vegetable section in your local supermarket should be labelled and promoted as prebiotic foods! We will also look at which vegetables reign supreme in promoting good microbes to flourish.

## *What about meat?*

Although animal protein doesn't have a negative impact on gut health, it doesn't promote better gut health either. Replacing meat with plant-based proteins means that you are ingesting more fibre, avoiding second-hand antibiotics and doing the planet a huge favour too. Choosing the balance between eating enough plant-based whole foods and meat is essential. The plant-based recipes in the chapter Prebiotic Plant-based Meals will provide you with an arsenal of fibre-rich recipes where meat will not even be missed.

## *On balance and being human*

We are all human and can't eat perfectly healthily 100% of the time. It would also be awfully yawn-yawn. There are sure to be times when you cannot resist that piece of refined wheat flour cake, or have the Sunday lunch with all the trimmings, and that is perfectly okay. After all, aren't we striving to be perfect in our imperfection?

Our main objective should be to eat healthily 90% of the time, and allow ourselves some naughty treats occasionally for three very important reasons:

- It's good for your soul!
- It reminds us how uncomfortable and less than healthy those foods/meals can make us feel.
- Most importantly, once your gut health is once again thriving you can afford to break the rules occasionally and your body will cope with your choice of treat quite well.

## *Getting back on the wagon*

After a particularly bad meal choice or day it's a good idea to start the next day with an intermittent fasting morning. Intermittent fasting sounds extreme, but it simply means that you don't have any solid food until 12 pm; a smoothie and a 'bulletproof' coffee (explained in my **Gentle Start Suggestions**) will assist in getting you through the morning, then at lunch it is important to choose a healthy plant-based meal.

## Prepare for a healing crisis

When you start out on this path to your best gut health, there will be an adjustment period for your digestive system to get used to all the fibre. Symptoms may include bloating, a runny tummy, cramps, etc. You may experience some discomfort for a week or two, but it does pass. See page 27 for my **Gentle Start** Suggestions that you can follow to reduce these 'healing crisis' symptoms.

# Foods for a thriving gut

In a nutshell, the key to your best gut health lies in eating a wide variety of vegetables and other fibre-rich plant-based foods daily – and lots of it. In order for your microbes to thrive and multiply they need food (prebiotics). The best kind of food for your gut bugs are *rich in inulin or resistant starches*, but to keep it simple let's refer to them as 'prebiotics'. All vegetables, fruits and other plant-based foods such as beans, lentils and whole grains contain prebiotics; some more than others.

Below is a list of plant-based foods that are prebiotic rock stars:

- Green bananas (and green banana flour for baking)
- Peas
- Lentils
- Whole rolled oats
- Cannellini beans
- Inulin
- Artichokes
- Asparagus
- Onions
- Leeks
- Garlic

## Other good food choices for flourishing (gut) health

- When purchasing eggs, dairy, red meat, poultry and pork products, look out for the words pasture fed or free range, as well as an assurance on the labelling that the animals received no routine antibiotic treatments or growth hormones.
- When using salt, stick to Pink Himalayan salt or unprocessed sea salt.
- Bone broth is a wonderful and delicious gut healing stock that is rich in gelatine and minerals to assist in

healing leaky gut syndrome and nourishes your body and joints too. Aim to include bone broth into your diet as often as possible. I have included two broth recipes from Marrow in the chapter Healing Soups & Broths. You can add broth to any soup or stew, or even cook brown rice and quinoa in broth and add it to salads, or as a side dish to a plant-based stew.

- Oils & fats: Ghee or butter from grass/pasture fed cows is a good addition (in moderation) to a healthy diet. Ghee can be used for low temperature sautéing and baking with delicious results. Coconut oil and macadamia oil are my two favourite high-temperature cooking oils; they are rich in good fats and much better for you than sunflower or canola oil (which should be avoided where possible). Cold-pressed olive oil should only be used as a dressing or in pesto and other cold dips and sauces as it becomes toxic at high temperatures.

- Lentils & beans are wonderful food for your microbes, but may cause some discomfort if suddenly introduced to your diet. I recommend avoiding them for the first two weeks during your gut-healing journey, and then gradually introducing them. Make sure that all lentils and beans (and even wholegrains) are soaked overnight (and the soaking water discarded) before cooking them well in salted water to avoid bloating or digestive discomfort. The spices 'hing' and ground coriander can be added to lentil and bean dishes to further reduce any digestive discomfort.

- Learn to enjoy the skin of roasted vegetables such as sweet potatoes, potatoes and butternut; they serve as wonderful food for your microbes. The stalky parts of vegetables such as asparagus, broccoli and cauliflower are also fabulously fibre-rich and should be eaten with enthusiasm.

- When it comes to purchasing readymade products I really rate the following ones that are made from the best ingredients and are all natural: **Kerrygold** butter and cheese made from grass fed cows; **Pesto Princess** pesto's and sauces; **The Health Connection**'s nutritional yeast, gluten free whole rolled oats, and Superfood Powders; **Solgar**'s or **Nature's Choice** deactivated brewer's yeast; and **Spice and All Things Nice**'s curry pastes. Most of these products can be found at your local **Wellness Warehouse**, or ordered online from them.

- The 'good carb, bad carb' explained: For good gut health, whole grains and high-carb vegetables can be most beneficial. I enjoy **Santa Anna**'s Organic Wholegrain and non-GMO corn chips and tortillas, Nature's Choice non-GMO popcorn kernels, **The Health Connection**'s gluten free whole rolled oats, as well as roasted sweet potatoes, baked white potatoes (occasionally), brown basmati rice, wholegrain soba (buckwheat) noodles and pulse pastas as part of a healthy gut healing diet.

It is also important to remember that a healthy gut and body needs a wide variety of plant-based foods. Remember to include as many colours (green, red, yellow, white, orange and purple veggies) daily into your diet to make sure you are getting all the nutrients you need.

As discussed in detail in my first book, *The Yoga Kitchen*, I recommend that when you are addressing weight-loss, high starch vegetables such as potatoes, butternut and sweet potatoes as well as starchy grains (albeit whole grains) should not be combined with animal proteins. An example would be that when enjoying a fillet of fish or beef, etc., your side dishes should be low-carbs such as quinoa, salad and watery (non-starchy) vegetables, like broccoli, cauliflower, onions, tomatoes, cabbage, aubergines, leeks, asparagus, spinach, etc.

## On being brave

To wrap things up, the wonderful news about restoring your gut health is that it's never too late.

The best way to go about transforming your (gut) health to your best (gut) health is to return to the kitchen. Cooking from scratch with ingredients that are food for good bacteria is the only way to avoid processed or convenience meals lacking in essential fibre, enzymes and nutrients, and to ensure that you stay on the path to thriving long-term health.

To live a ferociously healthy, happy and meaningful life, you will need to make changes. But shifts and transformation are uncomfortable. If you want to transform your health, adjust your expectations and prepare yourself for a time of discomfort. If you expect it and allow it, you have a far better chance of achieving your health goals, and remember that failure is an important part of every transformation.

Starting with what you are choosing to eat is a huge step in the right direction to living your best life; clear out the pantry (throw away any product your great granny wouldn't recognise as food). Rearrange your kitchen and make it a calm and happy space where you want to hang out. Spoil yourself with some gorgeous bowls and platters that will inspire you to fill them with delicious and nourishing food. Find some time to plan menus ahead, count colours on your plate instead of calories and make some time to become more mindful and experience every mouthful of your delicious, love-filled, homemade meals.

Discard your old, tired habits and create new ones. Join an evening cooking class, or Google a 'How To' and start a new project at home (I recommend fermenting your own vegetables, sourdough baking and swearing silently – all very therapeutic). Choose a positive community to surround yourself with and allow them to inspire you, let go of the ones who are enabling your bad habits (this may mean being ruthless in your pursuit to change the landscape of your life). Clear out some of the old to make room for the new. And above all, be brave.

Happy cooking and healing.

# Gentle Start Suggestions

On the following page are some recipes that are perfect
as an introduction to eating for great gut health.

# Gentle Start Suggestions

## Mornings

### Intermittent fasting

Although this term sounds fraught with hunger pangs, in reality it is far less extreme or uncomfortable. It simply means that you won't be eating solids for a couple of mornings a week (and not on consecutive days) to allow your digestive tract the healing time it needs and specifically introducing ingredients like gelatine during these fasting mornings to assist gut healing. Having a smoothie or a cup of broth will keep hunger at bay until lunch time and make you feel energetic and light.

A smoothie and/or a cup of broth along with a bulletproof coffee will get you through the morning. The smoothie will provide the essential fibre your microbes need. The bulletproof coffee consists of filtered or real brewed coffee (choose lightly roasted beans, which contain more antioxidants), add a heaped teaspoon of grass-fed ghee or coconut oil to it instead of milk, mix well and enjoy. Of course you can omit the coffee, but I for one am simply not human until I've had a cup. The broth is especially helpful for healing the gut on a fasting morning while the digestive system is at rest.

I recommend:

- Smoothies (see pages 48–49)
- Marrow Broths (see pages 82–83)
- Overnight Oats (see page 44)

## Lunch

During your gentle start, a soup for lunch is a great idea, easy to digest but with tonnes of fibre to keep your microbes happy. I also recommend combining it with a simple salad of leafy greens (dressed with olive oil and lemon juice) to add enzymes and additional nutrients. Leafy greens are easy to digest too. A little side helping of fermented veggies will not only make your meal more delicious, but also introduce a wider spectrum of good microbes to your gut.

- Carrot, Apple & Ginger Soup (see page 66)
- Pea & Miso Soup (see page 74)
- Guru Ramdas Yoga Retreat Soup (see page 68)

- Spinach, Sweet Potato & Red Lentil Soup (see page 72)
- Beetroot Bliss (see page 70)

## Supper

Including some more fabulous fibre at supper time is essential to ensure that your good microbes are multiplying and establishing themselves properly. Sticking to cooked vegetables makes digestion easier, but again, as with lunch, include a leafy green side salad to add enzymes as well as some golden sauerkraut or pickled onions to add prebiotics and probiotics.

- Middle Eastern Butternut Stew (see page 120)
- Simple Egg Fried Rice (see page 136)
- Chicken, Leek & Cannellini Bean Stew (see page 148)
- Glorious Oven-roasted Cabbage & Bacon (see page 158)
- Massaman Curry (see page 118)
- Moussaka (see page 144)

## Something Sweet

During your gentle start, homemade jellies, stewed apples as well as dark chocolate (at least 85% cocoa solids or more) can be enjoyed to satisfy your sweet cravings and assist in the healing process.

- Rooibos & Lemon Jelly (see page 166)
- Raspberry & Yoghurt Mousse (see page 169)
- Apple Stew Crumble (see page 168)

## Drinks

Avoid alcohol during your gut-healing gentle start, and instead enjoy a lovely glass of Kombucha in the evenings (see page 89).

Coffee and tea are permitted, but with no sugar and just a little A2 milk or with a milk alternative (not soy).

Apart from the above, stick to green tea and filtered water.

Note: You can get in touch via the www.yogakitchen.co.za for a personalised plan.

# Good Morning Sunshine

## Breakfast/brunch meals for good gut health

### INTRODUCTION

*On breakfast & being a good egg*

Every morning is a fresh chance to set the tone for good food choices. When you make the right breakfast/brunch choices you are bound to continue with microbe-friendly food choices throughout the day.

As someone who leans more towards a plant-based diet, eggs to me really are a wonderful food crammed with excellent nutrition as well as tonnes of protein. In this chapter, Good Morning Sunshine, I have included some of my favourite egg dishes that will delight your taste buds, as well as some fibre-rich recipes that will feed your microbes and keep you going until lunch time.

I wish you glorious mornings ahead and plenty of good eggs along your path. Happy cooking!

# Labneh & Fried Eggs

I am always looking for interesting recipes with eggs as they are the perfect breakfast food. Combined with the live Greek yoghurt in this recipe, you also introduce beneficial gut-friendly probiotics to your diet.

*Herbed Greek yoghurt sauce*
1 cup Greek yoghurt
1 tbsp dill, finely chopped
1 tbsp mint, finely chopped
1 clove garlic, grated
⅓ tsp sea salt
¼ tsp freshly ground black pepper

*Eggs in chilli ghee*
1 heaped tbsp ghee or unsalted butter
1 tsp chilli flakes
½ tsp sweet paprika
⅛ tsp ground cumin
4 large eggs

*To dress up*
½ tbsp fresh mint, chopped
½ tbsp fresh dill, chopped
1 spring onion, finely chopped or sliced
salt and pepper to taste

*To make the herbed Greek yoghurt*

Evenly mix Greek yoghurt, chopped dill, mint, grated garlic, salt and ground black pepper together. Cover tight with plastic wrap and let it sit in the fridge for 1 hour.

*To cook the eggs in the chilli ghee*

Combine the ghee or unsalted butter, chilli flakes, paprika and ground cumin in a pan over medium heat, stirring continuously. Once the butter has melted, let the spices cook gently for another minute, then turn the heat up and break the eggs carefully into the chilli ghee mixture, place the lid on the pan and cook to your preference (I prefer soft and sunny side up).

Lastly serve the fried eggs and yoghurt on a plate in any manner that pleases you, sprinkling generously with the herbs and chopped spring onions.

# Superfood Breakfast

Serves 1

This breakfast is more about the combination of ingredients than a particular recipe. The sweet potato and greens together with eggs (or another protein of your choice) is nutrition dense, delicious and super-gut food for your microbes.

1 medium jewel (orange flesh) sweet
    potato
2 eggs
2–4 sprouting broccoli stems
2–4 asparagus stems
1 tsp tamari sauce
1 tsp toasted sesame oil
a handful of baby spinach (optional)
salt to taste

Start by roasting the sweet potato with the skin until it's soft; it will need approximately 45–60 minutes at 180°C.

Poach or boil the eggs to your preference.

Just before the sweet potatoes are ready, blanch the broccoli and asparagus for 4 minutes in salted boiling water, drain immediately. Serve together with the poached or boiled eggs. Season everything with tamari sauce, toasted sesame oil and salt before tucking in.

# The Hideaway Vegan Brunch Pancake

Serves 2

Stephen and Jackie from The Hideaway in Swellendam rustle up these delicious vegan pancakes for their yoga retreat brunches. When you are on a mission to avoid grain flours and eat more plant-based foods with plenty of gut-loving fibre, then this is a recipe you should get intimately acquainted with. In addition these pancakes are also grain (gluten) & dairy free – yay all the way!

½ cup chickpea flour (also known as chana or garbanzo flour)

¼ tsp garlic powder

¼ tsp fine-grain sea salt

⅛ tsp freshly ground black pepper

¼ tsp bicarbonate of soda

½ cup water

2 spring onions, finely chopped (about ¼ cup)

8 Portobello mushrooms, chopped

1–2 tbsp ghee or coconut oil

Add all the dry ingredients to a large mixing bowl and stir well. Then add the water until you have a thick batter-like mixture.

Fry the spring onions and mushrooms in the ghee or coconut oil until they start softening and browning.

Next add the chickpea batter to the pan, turn the heat to low and place a lid on the pan (skillet), allowing to slowly cook for about 5 minutes.

Carefully turn the pancake over using an egg flipper or spatula, allowing another 3 minutes cooking time before transferring it to a large plate or a platter dish.

Optional: Serve with some micro salad leaves, mashed avocado, chopped red onion and sauerkraut or any other fermented vegetable, and a grinding of salt and black pepper.

# Gutsy Frittata

For an excellent gut-health-promoting breakfast or brunch it will be difficult to match this fibre- and nutrient-dense breakfast. This is also a great lunchbox addition (see my Paleo Lunchbox Ideas on page 52).

⅔ cup baby peas
ghee or coconut oil for sautéing
4–6 slim spring onions
4–6 eggs
½ cup live Greek yoghurt
½ cup white cheddar
salt and pepper to taste

Preheat the oven to 180°C.

Start by blanching the peas for 3 minutes in boiling water, then drain and set aside.

In a pan melt some ghee or coconut oil on medium heat and add the spring onions, sautéing on medium heat until they start softening.

In a large mixing bowl beat the eggs well, then add the yoghurt and cheese and mix well.

Next, add the well-drained peas and sautéed spring onions to the egg mixture and season with salt and freshly ground pepper; then give it a good stir.

Transfer the mixture to a greased (with ghee/coconut oil), fairly deep, square or round baking tin and bake for 15 minutes. Allow to cool a little before serving.

Serve with a leafy green salad and freshly ground black pepper.

Lunchbox tip: If making these for lunchboxes, divide your mixture into equal portions in a greased muffin tin and bake. They can be stored for up to 3 days in the fridge.

# Jackie's Paleo Granola

Makes 20 portions

This recipe has been generously shared by my friend, fellow yogi, generally angelic and lovely human Jackie Young (co-owner at The Hideaway Guesthouse in Swellendam).

As part of a retreat brunch, Jackie prepares this sublime granola and everyone always wants the recipe afterwards. It is completely grain/gluten free, vegan and packed with good fats and fibre to keep you going well past lunchtime. For another Hideaway Retreat brunch recipe, check out The Hideaway Vegan Brunch Pancake (see page 36).

2 cups raw walnuts

2 cups raw cashews

1 cup raw pumpkin seeds

1 cup unsweetened shredded coconut

1 cup dried cranberries

½ cup sunflower seeds

½ cup sesame seeds

½ cup linseeds

⅓ cup coconut oil

⅓ cup honey or maple syrup

1 tsp vanilla extract

½ tsp ground cinnamon

½ tsp salt

Preheat the oven to 150°C.

Chop the nuts into small pieces, place in a deep roasting tin and add the pumpkin seeds, shredded coconut, cranberries, sunflower seeds, sesame seeds and linseeds.

In a large jug, combine the coconut oil, honey, vanilla extract, ground cinnamon and salt. Mix well.

Pour the oil and honey mixture over the nut, seed and fruit mixture and stir well to make sure that all the ingredients are well coated. Bake in the oven for 10–15 minutes.

Remove the mixture from the oven and stir well.

Return the mixture to the oven and bake for a further 10–15 minutes or until golden brown and crispy.

Remove the mixture from the oven and leave to cool for at least 10 minutes before stirring to allow the nut clusters to develop. (Use a spatula to get under the granola and release it from the bottom of the roasting tin.)

Once the mixture is completely cool, store in an airtight container.

Serve with coconut yoghurt and real maple syrup for a vegan option, or live dairy yoghurt and raw honey.

# Avocado, Bacon & Cannellini Brunch

Serves 2

Naturally smoked, pasture-fed pork can be a healthy addition to your diet from time to time as pasture-fed pork's fat is high in omega 3. In this recipe, the cannellini beans and avocado provide the gut-healthy fibre (prebiotics) while the pasture-fed bacon is a great source of omega 3. Make sure you also choose naturally smoked bacon. If you really want to go to town with fibre you can add some grilled tomatoes and sautéed mushrooms too.

1 cup cooked and drained cannellini
   beans
4 strips streaky bacon
1 ripe avocado
salt and pepper to taste
Blonde Pesto (see page 114)

Cannellini beans can be purchased in a can or jar; drain them well before using them. Alternatively you can soak dry beans overnight, then discard the soaking water in the morning, and cook them until tender in well-salted water. Drain well, then set aside.

Lay the bacon strips out on a baking tray and place it under a hot grill in your oven. It will need approximately 10–15 minutes to achieve the desired crispiness.

While the bacon is grilling, peal and slice the avocado.

Once the bacon is ready, remove it from the oven and drain the bacon fat into a pan, then add the cooked cannellini beans to the pan, season with salt and sauté them on high heat for a few minutes in the bacon fat.

Serve plated – sliced avocado, crispy bacon and sautéed cannellini beans with a grinding of fresh black pepper and salt to taste, and a drizzle of Blonde Pesto.

# Yoga Kitchen Overnight Oats

Soaked whole rolled oats provide wonderful food for your good bacteria as well as an excellent amount of energy to get through the morning.

1 cup whole rolled oats

1 cup coconut milk

1 cup filtered water

¼ cup almond butter (or cashew butter)

1 tsp cinnamon

¼ tsp salt

3 tbsp chia seeds

½ cup pitted dates, chopped

raw honey to serve

In a large bowl, mix all the ingredients together except the honey. Cover and store the bowl in the refrigerator overnight. The soaked oats can be stored in the fridge for up to 4 days.

Serve with a drizzle of raw honey, a sprinkle of chia seeds and some more dates.

# The Wellness Café Breakfast Wrap

Makes 2 wraps

Made from potato and chickpea flour, these wraps are full of fibre. They are available from most health shops – buy them in bulk and keep them in the freezer for convenience.

1 tsp coconut oil/ghee

8 brown or white mushrooms, quartered

½ tsp dried thyme

salt to taste

4 eggs, whisked well

2 potato and chickpea flour wraps

¼ cup cultured cream cheese

½ cup baby tomatoes, washed and sliced into quarters

½ cup wild rocket, washed and dried

In some ghee or coconut oil sauté the mushrooms with the thyme; season with salt. Once they are cooked, transfer them to a bowl and set aside.

In the same pan used for the mushrooms add some more ghee or coconut oil and cook the eggs as you would an omelette on medium heat, turning it over once carefully. Slide it onto a plate and set aside.

Next, heat the wraps in the same pan used for the egg omelette briefly (30 seconds each side). Remove them and place on separate plates. Spread the cream cheese over the top. Add the rest of the ingredients to the open flat wrap – halved omelette, tomatoes, rocket and mushrooms. Roll them close, cut them in thirds and enjoy.

# The Wellness Café Power up Smoothie

Serves 1

If you need a quick alkalising and nourishing boost, look no further than this yummy smoothie from the Wellness (Warehouse) Café. Hemp seeds contain over 30% fat. They are exceptionally rich in two essential fatty acids, linoleic acid (omega 6) and alpha-linolenic acid (omega 3). They also contain gamma-linolenic acid, which has been linked with several health benefits.

¼ raw hemp seeds
4 whole, pitted dates
2 tsp raw honey
1 tsp Wellness Warehouse alkaliser
3 cup almond milk
4–6 ice cubes

Add all the ingredients to your blender jug and whiz until you have a smooth consistency.

# Gutsy Oat Smoothie

Serves 2

Oats are high in beta-glucan, which is a soluble fibre with numerous benefits. It helps reduce cholesterol and blood sugar levels, promotes good gut bacteria and increases feelings of fullness.

Gluten-free, whole rolled or steel cut oats are one of the best grains to include as part of a gut-healthy diet. Oats is best when soaked overnight. You can count on this very filling smoothie to keep your energy levels stable throughout the morning.

2 greenish bananas (they should be on the cusp of becoming ripe; the less ripe a banana is the higher the resistant starch content in them)

¼ cup whole rolled oats, soaked overnight in ½ cup filtered water

1 cup baby spinach or kale

2 tbsp maca superfood powder

1 tsp chia seeds

1 cup almond or coconut milk

pinch cinnamon and drizzle of raw honey

Add all the above ingredients to your blender jug, and pulse/whiz until you have smooth mixture. Add some water if you prefer a runnier consistency.

# *Lunchbox Love*

## Gut-friendly food ideas for on the go

### INTRODUCTION

One of the biggest challenges to staying on track with a gut-healthy diet is choosing the right meals at work, or when on the run.

Most of the salad recipes included in the chapter Crunch & Cultured can be pre-prepared for lunchboxes, but to make life a bit easier I have added a few of my go-to lunch combos. Once you get into the habit of making and packing lunch boxes it will become quite effortless.

In fact, the mere act of preparing a delicious and nourishing lunch selection ahead for the coming week (while the rest of the world is watching television) will trigger a powerful sense of smugness and wellbeing.

# Paleo Lunchbox Ideas

## Egg Salad Paleo Box

Apple & nut butter: Simply add a tablespoon of nut butter to some sliced apple (a sprinkle of cinnamon can be added).

Avo & kale chips: 1 small avocado peeled and halved and sprinkled with kale chips (have a look at my *Yoga Kitchen* cookbook for a kale chip recipe, or simply buy some).

Egg salad: 2 boiled eggs served with some crunchy leaves and thinly sliced red onion; dress it simply with olive oil and lemon juice.

## Gutsy Frittata, Dried Mango and Sweet Potato Medallions with Sunflower Seed Spread

2 Gutsy Frittatas (see page 38)

3–4 pieces dried mango, or any other sulphur-free dried fruit

2 heaped tbsp Vegan Sunflower Seed Spread (see page 114) with roasted sweet potato medallions

Simply wash and scrub a few jewel (orange fleshed) sweet potatoes and then slice them in approximately 1.5 cm thick medallions, place them on a baking tray greased with coconut oil and roast them for 30 minutes at 180°C in a pre-heated oven. Allow to cool completely before storing them in the fridge in an airtight container.

# Plant-based Lunchbox Ideas

These plant-based, fibre-rich, gut-friendly lunchboxes can mostly be prepared ahead quite easily on a Sunday evening.

## Crunchy Vegan 1

Mashed avocado and sliced tomato on wholegrain rice cakes

Apple slices with nut butter and cinnamon

Roasted vegetables with pesto on salad leaves

Cut any roasting vegetables into large chunks (leaving the skin on where possible, for instance sweet potatoes and butternut). Season them with salt and roast them in an open baking tray in coconut oil – they will need more or less 50 minutes. Allow the veggies to cool completely before transferring them to the fridge in an airtight container. When adding them to your lunchbox, combine them with a dollop of pesto to add flavour.

## Crunchy Vegan 2

Combine the following yummy components for a lovely crunchy vegan lunchbox.

Quinoa Tabbouleh (see page 93)

Corn chips with Holy Guacamole (see page 115) or Sunflower Seed Spread (see page 114).

Granola Bars (see page 210).

# *School Lunchbox Ideas & Frittata Recipe*

When it comes to school lunchboxes, the key is to keep it new and interesting. Here are some ideas to make up healthy lunchbox combinations for kids.

Veggie sticks with hummus or Sunflower Seed Spread (see page 114)

Wholegrain rice cakes with nut butter and honey

Banana chips

Pulse Pastas (see page 192)

Sourdough Sarmies (see page 60)

French Toast Soldiers (see page 184)

Springbok or kudu biltong & air roasted nuts

## School Lunchbox Frittata

Makes 6

6 slices bacon, cut into small pieces
2 yellow or brown onions, finely diced
½ cup grated cheddar cheese
6 eggs
ghee for gressing
salt to taste

Preheat the oven to 180°C.

Start by frying the bacon and onion together in a cast-iron pan until the bacon is fairly crispy and the onions soft and golden. Take off the heat and set aside.

Beat the eggs and season them with salt.

Then simply combine all the ingredients in a mixing bowl and pour the mixture into a 6-partition muffin tin which has been greased with ghee.

Bake for 20 minutes. Serve immediately, or, if using these for lunchboxes, allow them to cool completely before storing them in an airtight container in the fridge.

# Sourdough Sarmies

Serves 1

For optimal gut health you should mostly avoid refined wheat flour foods, but let's be honest and admit that a world without sandwiches would plunge anyone into a deep and dark depression. Once you have restored your gut health to 'thriving mode' (see page 22 for my guidelines on how to get there) a true sourdough or even better a whole-wheat sourdough sandwich (made with unbleached, non-GMO wheat flour) can once again be enjoyed occasionally (once or twice a week). The added benefit of choosing sourdough bread is that the gluten content diminishes during the leavening and baking processes, and undesirable ingredients such as instant yeast, preservatives and trans-fats can also avoided.

The following sourdough sarmies will keep hunger at bay until supper time with plenty of fibre to feed your microbes.

# Avocado, Kimchi & Roasted Sweet Potato Sarmie

1 small mashed avocado, seasoned with a
little salt
4–6 roasted sweet potato medallions (see
page 52)
1–2 tbsp kimchi

Simply 'butter' 2 slices of whole-wheat sourdough with
your avocado mash, arrange the sweet potato medallions
on one of the slices and then add the kimchi evenly over the
medallions. Complete the sandwich with the other slice and
wrap it securely for your lunchbox. Keep it in the fridge until
it's time to tuck in.

# Good Old Hummus & Salad Sarmie

¼ cup hummus
red cabbage, thinly sliced
red pepper, thinly sliced
3–4 whole leaf butter lettuce or any other
kind of your choice

Simply 'butter' 2 slices of whole-wheat sourdough with a
thick layer of hummus, arrange the cabbage and red pepper
on one of the slices, and then lastly add the lettuce leaves on
top. Complete the sandwich with the other slice and wrap it
well for your lunchbox. Keep it in the fridge until it's time to
tuck into it.

# Roasted Veg & Pesto Sarmie

2 tbsp pesto
a medley of roasted courgette, sweet
potato & red onion
lettuce leaves of your choice
red cabbage, thinly sliced

Simply 'butter' 2 slices of whole-wheat sourdough with a
substantial layer of pesto, arrange the roasted veggies on
one of the slices, and then add the lettuce leaves on top of
the veggies. Complete the sandwich with the other slice and
wrap it ready for your lunchbox. Keep it in the fridge until it's
time to tuck in.

# Egg, Mayo, Spinach & Branston Pickle Sarmie

While living in the UK I met a delightfully eccentric French girl with skin like porcelain and a mouth like a sailor. She had exquisite taste in clothes, art, food and wine, but religiously started her day with the following sandwich from the local 'caff' near where we worked. This particular sandwich made no sense to me until I took my first bite, after which I was hooked too.

2 hardboiled eggs
1 heaped tbsp Hellman's mayonnaise
pink or sea salt to taste
A good handful of baby spinach
1 tbsp fine Branston Pickle

Mash the eggs and mayonnaise together, adding a little pink or sea salt to taste, and then spread both slices with a generous layer of egg and mayo. On one of the slices arrange the spinach and on the other a thin layer of Branston pickle and then join them together in holy matrimony of the taste buds. Wrap, and store in the fridge until it's time to eat.

# Healing Broths & Soups

## Soothing soups and broths for gut healing

### INTRODUCTION

Eating of soup is one of the best ways to start your gut-healing journey and a good time to start is during the colder months. Choosing a light breakfast and then a soup for lunch and a stew for supper is a great way to allow your digestive system to rest and heal when the right foods, such as soups with easily digestible cooked vegetables (fibre), are consumed.

You will also notice that I have included bone broth in most of the soup recipes. Bone broth is rich in gelatine and nutrients that will assist in healing the little perforations in your gut lining caused by refined flour foods.

Marrow, the first bone broth bar in Cape Town, has generously shared two of their delicious bone broth recipes (see pages 82 and 83). Replacing one of your morning cups of coffee with a cup of bone broth, especially on a fasting morning, will put your gut-healing journey on the fast track. See my Gentle Start Suggestions on page 27 for more information on intermittent fasting and healing your gut.

# Carrot, Apple & Ginger Soup

Serves 2

Cooked apples are an excellent source of pectin, which is a non-starch polysaccharide that is difficult to digest, providing food for colonic bacteria that convert it into beneficial short-chain fatty acids. These acids maintain the health of beneficial gut bugs and the cells lining the colon. Short-chain fatty acids also promote epithelial growth of the cells of the intestines, thereby reducing leaky gut. Pectin also help to normalise intestinal contractions and is therefore good for preventing diarrhoea or constipation. Pectin even binds with and eliminates some heavy metals from your body.

In addition, ginger and carrots are great sources of nutrition, and the flavours of these three ingredients work exceptionally well together.

6 Granny Smith apples (but really any variety will work), peeled and cored

6 medium carrots, unpeeled but scrubbed and topped and tailed

1–2 thumb-sized pieces of fresh ginger, finely grated

1 heaped tsp turmeric

2 cups vegetable stock or chicken broth (see page 83)

salt to taste

black pepper and a sprinkle of chia seeds to garnish

Cut the apples and carrots into big chunks and then add them to your soup pot along with all the other ingredients. Bring to the boil and then turn down the heat. Simmer for 45 minutes with the lid on.

Once the carrots and apples are tender, remove the pot from the heat and allow to cool for 5 minutes before whizzing it into a silky consistency with your hand blender.

Serve simply with a generous grinding of black pepper and chia seeds.

# Guru Ramdas Yoga Retreat Soup

Serves 4–8

I was honoured to cater a retreat for the sublime Guru Ramdas Yoga Studio recently. This soup was devised after one of the lovely participants contributed some oranges to my kitchen. I was planning on just making a fairly simple pumpkin soup and suddenly the addition of juiced oranges and seeds seemed like a good idea. In addition, I was treated to the sounds of beautiful chanting throughout the retreat while I prepared their meals. I love my job! For more information on Guru Ramdas yoga retreats or teacher training, visit http://www.gururamdas.co.za/

Pumpkin is an excellent source of fibre, which is food for your microbes. Tasty and crunchy, pumpkin seeds are high in zinc, an important nutrient for digestive enzyme production and immune system function. Sunflower seeds promotes cardiovascular health and healthy cholesterol levels, is a potent source of magnesium and Selenium, the former being a powerful antioxidant to boot.

1 tbsp ghee or coconut oil

2 medium brown or yellow onions, roughly chopped

3 cups pumpkin, cubed & peeled (white skinned pumpkin works well, but any squash or pumpkin variety will work)

3 oranges, juiced

salt and pepper to taste

1 tsp coriander powder

1 tsp turmeric

3 cups vegetable stock

½ cup sunflower seeds, lightly toasted

½ cup pumpkin seeds (pepitas), lightly toasted

olive oil for serving

Sauté the onions in the ghee or coconut oil until soft and translucent, then add the cubed pumpkin and continue sautéing the cubes together with the onions in the pot.

Add the orange juice, salt, pepper, coriander powder, turmeric and stock, and allow to simmer on low heat for 1 hour.

In the meantime, lightly toast the seeds in a dry pan on low heat, stirring frequently. Set them aside in a plate to cool.

After a full hour of cooking the pumpkin and stock mixture, take the pot off the heat and add most of the seeds, just keeping a handful back for garnishing.

Using a hand blender, whiz the soup until you have a fairly smooth consistency.

Serve with a sprinkle of seeds and a drizzle of olive oil.

# Beetroot Bliss

Beetroot is a powerhouse of gut-healthy fibre and antioxidants. The amino acid glutamine that is abundant in beetroot assists in maintaining a healthy digestive tract.

8 medium beetroot, washed, topped and tailed, then quartered
½ tsp chilli flakes (dried chilli)
2 cups vegetable stock, or chicken broth
salt to taste
¼ cup coconut cream for garnishing (optional)
Coconut Dukah to garnish (see page 112)

Add all the ingredients apart from the coconut cream and dukah to a soup pot and bring to the boil, then reduce the heat and allow to simmer for approximately 1 hour.

Take the pot off the heat, allow to cool for 5 minutes, and then blitz to a silky smooth consistency with your hand blender.

Serve with a swirl of coconut cream and a sprinkling of crunchy Coconut Dukah.

# Spinach, Sweet Potato & Red Lentil Soup

Serves 4–8

This soup is full of prebiotic fibre for your good gut flora to feast on. Soaking the lentils overnight and then draining and rinsing them well before cooking them will aid digestion. Lentils are high in protein and fibre, and sweet potatoes (especially the orange-fleshed variety) are rich in wonderful vitamins, minerals and phytonutrients as well as being fibre rich.

2 tsp coconut oil

1 large yellow/brown onion, finely chopped

2 cloves garlic, finely grated or crushed

½ cup red split lentils, preferably soaked overnight in some water

3 medium jewel (orange fleshed) sweet potatoes, grated

2 tsp turmeric

1 tsp cumin

1 tsp garam masala

½ tsp cinnamon

3 cups vegetable stock or chicken/beef bone broth

salt and pepper to taste

2–3 cups baby spinach, washed and dried

olive oil and nutritional yeast flakes to garnish (optional)

Sauté the onion in coconut oil until it is soft and fragrant. Add the garlic, well-drained lentils, grated sweet potato, spices, salt and pepper. Sauté for another minute and then add the stock or broth.

Allow to simmer on low heat for 50 minutes, then add the spinach, and let it simmer for a further 10 minutes.

Before serving give it a good whiz with your hand blender for a smooth, creamy consistency.

Serve with a drizzle of olive oil and a sprinkle of nutritional yeast.

# Pea & Miso Soup

Serves 4

Miso is rich in essential minerals and a good source of various B vitamins, vitamins E and K and folic acid. As a fermented food, miso provides the gut with beneficial bacteria. Green peas are a very good source of vitamin K, manganese, dietary fibre (prebiotic for your microbes), vitamin B1, copper, vitamin C, phosphorus and folate. They are also a good source of vitamin B6, niacin, vitamin B2, molybdenum, zinc, protein, magnesium, iron, potassium and choline. In addition, leeks are a super prebiotic food for your microbes.

Since children are either passionately crazy about peas or ferociously opposed to them (I have one of each) this smooth pea soup is a fabulous meal to fool the latter.

1 tsp coconut oil
10 stalks of baby leeks, finely sliced
4 cloves garlic, crushed
3 cups frozen green peas
2 tbsp miso paste (live, unpasteurised)
4 cups vegetable stock or chicken bone broth
1 (250 ml) tin coconut cream
salt to taste

Sauté the spring onions in the coconut oil; after 2 minutes add the garlic and continue sautéing for another 2 minutes or so.

Add all the remaining ingredients and simmer together for 15 minutes. Take the pot off the heat and allow to cool for 5 minutes before blitzing with a hand blender to a silky consistency.

Garnish with a drizzle of coconut cream (optional) and serve.

# Pho

Pho is a traditional Vietnamese soup. It is a wonderful immune booster and also easy to digest which makes it perfect for the start of your gut-healing journey. Pho is often confused with other Asian brothy meals like the Korean 'Guksu' and the Japanese 'Ramen'. The difference is that to make pho, the broth is gently simmered with the ingredients to ensure the soupy liquid remains clear while the others require rapid boiling.

## Beef Pho
Serves 4

1 thumb-size piece of ginger, julienned
6 spring onions, roughly chopped
1½ tsp coriander seeds
1 whole clove
1 tsp brown sugar
3 cups beef (or chicken) bone broth
2 tsp fish sauce
1 cup water
200–300 g fillet steak (use from frozen to make it easier to slice it thinly)
1 packet wholegrain soba noodles
salt and pepper to taste

*For the garnish*
¼ cup fresh mint, chopped
¼ cup fresh basil, chopped
¼ cup coriander leaves, chopped

tamari sauce or unpasteurised miso paste
juice of 2 limes
red chilli, thinly sliced (optional)

Add the ginger sticks, roughly chopped spring onions, coriander seeds, cloves and sugar into a deep soup pot and then pour in the broth and water. Add the fish sauce and bring it all to a gentle simmer over medium heat for about 30 minutes.

Meanwhile, prepare the garnish and the beef, slicing the frozen beef fillet with a very sharp knife against the grain into wafer-thin pieces.

Cook the soba noodles in well-salted water until al dente, then drain and rinse in cold water to stop them from sticking together, leaving them in the colander to continue draining.

Arrange the beef artfully into 4 bowls, then divide the cooked soba noodles equally into each bowl, and lastly strain about 1¼ cups of piping hot Pho broth over and meat and noodles, taking care that no spices from the simmering broth make their way into the bowls.

Garnish each bowl with equal amount of fresh herbs, a splash of tamari sauce or 1 teaspoon miso paste, lime juice and sliced chilli.

# Salmon Pho

Serves 4

*Salmon marinade*
1 clove garlic, grated
1 tbsp honey
2 tbsp soy sauce
½ lime, juice and zest
salt to taste

2 wild-caught salmon fillets (use from
   frozen)

6 spring onions, finely sliced
1 thumb-size piece of ginger, unpeeled,
   julienned
4 cups chicken broth
1 yellow onion, quartered
2 cups water
2 pods star anise
1 stick cinnamon
2 tbsp fish sauce
4 baby bok choy
2 cups courgette (zucchini) noodles
salt and pepper to taste
2 limes, juiced
½ cup fresh basil, chopped

Place all ingredients for the salmon marinade in a shallow bowl and mix well. Then thinly slice the salmon and add it to the marinade for 1 hour, turning over often.

Meanwhile, in a deep soup pot, sauté half the chopped spring onions and all of the ginger for about 4 minutes.

Add the broth, quartered onion, water, star anise and cinnamon, reduce the heat and gently simmer for about 30 minutes.

Add the fish sauce, bok choy, courgette noodles, salt and black pepper to the broth and allow to simmer for a further 8 minutes.

Pick out and discard the ginger, star anise and cinnamon stick from the broth.

To serve, scoop out and divide the courgette noodles and bok choy from the broth into 4 bowls, divide the marinated salmon between them and then pour the piping hot broth into each bowl. The salmon will gently start poaching and be wonderfully tender.

Serve with a good squeeze of lime juice, drizzle of leftover marinade and chopped basil into each bowl.

# Tuscan Cannellini Bean Soup

Cannellini beans contain both insoluble and soluble fibres, which offer many health benefits. Such is the fibre content that 200 grams of cooked cannellini beans can complete a whopping 50% of your daily recommended intake of dietary fibre. While insoluble fibre helps prevent digestive problems like irritable bowel syndrome, soluble fibre removes toxins from the body by binding to cholesterol-containing bile. They are also wonderfully nutty in taste and fluffy in texture.

1 tbsp butter or ghee
1 red onion, finely chopped
1 courgette (zucchini) grated
2 stalks celery, finely chopped with
    leaves
4 carrots, peeled and grated
3 cloves garlic, crushed or finely
    grated
4 cups bone broth (chicken or beef)
3 cups chopped baby spinach or kale
handful of fresh basil, finely chopped
1 cup tomato passata, or chopped Roma
    tomatoes
1 cup cooked, and drained cannellini
    beans
salt and pepper to taste
olive oil to serve

Heat the ghee/butter in a soup pot, add the onions, grated courgette and celery and sauté for about 20 minutes on very low heat until tender and golden. Add the carrots and garlic and sauté for another 5 minutes, stirring every now and again.

Add the broth and season with salt, then continue cooking on medium heat for another 30 minutes. Next add the spinach, basil, tomato passata and cannellini beans, and allow to simmer on low heat for a further 30 minutes.

Serve with a generous drizzle of olive oil and a good grinding of black pepper.

# Moroccan Lentil Soup

Serves 4–6

This soup is pure comfort food in colder weather. To ensure optimal digestion, soak the lentils overnight, then rinse and drain them well before adding them to the soup. They are wonderful food for your microbes and have plenty of protein.

1 tbsp ghee or butter (use coconut oil for a vegan option)

1 yellow/brown onion, peeled and diced

4 large carrots, peeled and diced

4 cloves garlic, peeled and minced

4 cups chicken broth (or vegetable stock for a vegan option)

1 cup black or brown lentils, soaked overnight

1¼ cup fresh, chopped tomatoes or 250 ml tomato passata

3 tbsp tomato paste

1 tsp ground cumin

1 tsp turmeric

½ tsp ground cinnamon

1 tsp ginger, freshly grated (or ground)

1 pinch cayenne pepper

juice of one fresh lemon or lime

salt and black pepper to taste

¼ cup fresh coriander leaves, chopped

olive oil for drizzling

Heat the ghee or butter in a large soup or stockpot over medium-high heat. Add the onion and carrots, and sauté for 5 minutes, stirring occasionally, until the onion is soft and translucent.

Add the garlic and sauté for a further minute, then add the broth or vegetable stock, drained lentils, tomatoes/passata, tomato paste, cumin, turmeric, cinnamon, ginger, cayenne pepper and lemon/lime juice.

Season well with salt and black pepper and then allow to cook on a low heat for at least 60–80 minutes.

Serve garnished with fresh coriander leaves and freshly ground black pepper and a generous drizzle of olive oil.

# Broth

Marrow, the first bone broth bar in Cape Town, makes these delicious and super nutritious broths that you can recreate easily at home. When making broth at home, a pressure cooker is essential and you can be creative with your spices and seasoning to suit your preferences, but always remember to add some raw apple cider vinegar, which helps to draw out the gelatine and minerals from the bones. Using a chicken carcass will reduce your cooking time considerably as the bones are much softer and more porous.

## Marrow Vegetable Broth

Makes 6 litres (12 individual servings)

500 g carrots, peeled and chopped

1 bunch celery, leaves removed and chopped

25 g parsley

2 green peppers, deseeded and chopped

800 g onion, sliced

60 g ginger, sliced

20 g galangal

1 head garlic

6 litres water

Place all of the ingredients in a large pot and bring to the boil. Once boiling, reduce to a simmer and cook for 1 hour.

Strain the broth and allow to cool. You can then divide the broth into 2, or even up to 12 portions (depending on your needs) and freeze for future use.

# Marrow Bone Broth

Makes 6 litres (12 individual servings)

2–3 carrots, peeled, but kept whole

2 onions, peeled and quartered

½ bunch celery, chopped into large
   pieces with the leaves

1 bulb garlic, peeled and chopped very
   roughly

¼ cup parsley (no chopping required)

1.5 kg bones (marrow, knuckles, beef
   stock bones)

4 chicken feet

5 bay leaves

10 pepper corns

50 ml apple cider vinegar

5 litres water

salt to taste

soy sauce/tamari

Simply add all the above ingredients to your large stock/soup pot and then bring it to a simmer and then allow cooking just below boiling point for 24–48 hours.

Allow the broth to cool completely before straining. Use a muslin cloth to strain the broth into another large pot or container. You can use ice packs to cool the broth down quickly.

Then divide the broth into 2, or even up to 12 portions (depending on your needs) and freeze for future use.

*When serving, use salt and soy sauce or tamari to season the broth. Just add enough to taste.*

# Crunch & Cultured

## Probiotic, fibre & enzyme rich salads for gut health

### INTRODUCTION

For your best gut health it is important to include an abundance of plant-based and fermented foods into your daily diet. In this chapter I have tried to combine both in most recipes.

I am a firm believer that any raw vegetable can be delicious when combined with a yummy sauce or dressing. In this chapter I have endeavoured to include recipes that are rich in both prebiotic and probiotic ingredients, and hope to demonstrate that culturing your own vegetables or throwing a healthy salad together can be fairly effortless with delicious and nourishing results.

Apart from the abundance of fibre you will be providing your good microbes with, salads also add a fabulous amount of excellent nutrients and enzymes to your diet.

For me lunch is the best time to enjoy salads. They can easily be prepared in the morning and packed into a lunchbox to enjoy later in the day.

# *Cultured Vegetables & Drinks*

## Probiotic & Prebiotic Pickled Onions

Makes 2 x 500 ml jars

4–5 red onions
1 tbsp sea salt
3–4 cups purified water
1 stick cinnamon per jar
2 cloves per jar
2 x 500 ml jars

Slice the onions in a food processor or by hand and place them in a mason jar. You may need more than one jar, depending on how many onions you use.

Heat ½ cup of water and add the salt to it. Stir until the salt dissolves. Add the rest of the cold water to the salt mixture. Once the brine has cooled to room temperature, add to the jar(s) with the onions, cinnamon stick and cloves. Make sure the onions are completely covered in the brine. Cover and let sit on the counter for 5–7 days before placing in the refrigerator.

Note: Taste the onions as they ferment and place them in the fridge once they have developed a flavour that you like. I usually taste them after 4 or 5 days and then leave them out longer if I want them to develop a more tart, pickled flavour. These will last in your fridge for up to a year.

# Golden Sauerkraut

1 green cabbages (save some of the outer
    layers of the cabbage for packaging on
    the top)
3 cups of grated carrots
1½ tsp grated ginger
1 tbsp fresh grated turmeric
1 tbsp ground turmeric
1 tbsp fennel seeds
2 tbsp salt

Wash the cabbage and scrub the carrots, then finely slice the cabbage and grate the carrots. Or use a food processor with a fine slicer attachment for the cabbage and rough grating attachment for the carrots.

Place all ingredients in a large mixing bowl. Use your hands (you might want to wear rubber gloves to prevent your hands getting stained by the turmeric) to mix and massage until it starts to get soft and juicy. The vegetables should release quite a lot of juice; if not, just add some more salt. Spoon the mixture into the clean jars.

Pack it really tightly to seal out all the air; keep packing until the jar is full and the veggies are covered in juice (important). Leave some space to place a whole folded cabbage leaf on top; this is to prevent any oxidation. Close with an air-tight lid.

During the fermentation process, the veggies will expand, pushing the liquid out. We put our jars in a bowl or a plastic bag to catch any juice that might drip from the sides. Leave the jars to ferment at room temperature for 1–2 weeks (depending on room temperature). When ready, your sauerkraut should be softly textured but not mushy and have a fresh, spicy and acidic flavour. Discard the cabbage leaf at the top and store the jars in the fridge.

Note: Use organic vegetables for fermenting and don't wash or scrub too much, it can destroy the natural microbes on the vegetables.

# The Good Gut's Simple Homemade Yoghurt

Makes 6 generous portions

I am sharing this simple homemade yoghurt recipe from the authors of *The Good Gut*, Erica and Justin Sonnenburg, who introduces it as follows: "Yoghurt with live probiotic cultures can easily be made at home at a fraction of the cost of store-bought versions; in addition you can also be more selective with the milk you use. I prefer using A2 milk now easily available from health food stores."

1 litre A2 whole milk
Approximately ¼ cup live yoghurt

Heat the milk in a medium saucepan to 80°C while occasionally stirring. Carefully monitor the temperature of the milk so that it doesn't boil over or scald. Once it has reached the correct temperature, remove the pan from the heat and allow the milk to cool to 45°C. Add the yoghurt to the warm milk, whisk, and transfer to a 1-litre mason jar and close the lid tightly. Place the jar in a yoghurt maker or an insulated cooler with enough warm water (40–45°C) so that the jar is sitting in about 5 cm of water. Leave the yoghurt overnight to ferment, and then put it in the refrigerator the next morning to firm up.

# Green Rooibos & Cinnamon Kombucha

Makes 6–8 portions

Kombucha is a traditionally fermented tea that, like all fermented foods, is extraordinarily rich in beneficial bacteria – those same bacteria that help to support gut health and immune system function. And, like most fermented foods, kombucha is blessedly simple to make – requiring little more effort or knowledge than you'd need in making a simple sweet tea. Kombucha is brewed and fermented by the way of a scoby, or a symbiotic colony of bacteria and yeasts – this is also referred to as a mother.

1 black teabags & 2 green rooibos
   teabags
2 litres filtered water
½ cup brown sugar
1 scoby
1 stick cinnamon
large jar
muslin cloth
elastic band

Using all the teabags, brew a strong tea in boiling water, adding the sugar and stirring until it is dissolved. Allow it to cool completely.

Add it to your storage jar once cooled, together with the scoby and cinnamon stick, cover with the muslin cloth fastened over the rim with the elastic band and allow at least 3–4 days of fermenting before consuming.

The longer you leave it the less sugary it will be, and the fizzier.

# Happy Gut Salad

1 cup cooked quinoa

1 carrot, julienned or grated

3 spring onions, thinly sliced

¼ cup pomegranate seeds

2 boiled and cooled eggs

½ cup kale chips

*For the dressing*

100 ml live Greek yoghurt

juice and zest of 1 small lemon

2 tbsp chopped mint

1 clove garlic, crushed

salt to taste

Mix together all the dressing ingredients in a jar to make a yoghurt sauce.

Add all the salad ingredients, apart from the boiled egg and kale chips, to a bowl, dress with the yoghurt sauce and garnish with the boiled, halved egg and crushed kale chips.

# Quinoa Tabbouleh

¾ cup quinoa (red or white, or mixed)

1 small Mediterranean cucumber, finely chopped

¼ cup parsley, finely chopped

¼ cup fresh mint, finely chopped

½ cup pomegranate seeds

¼ cup cold-pressed olive oil

1 tsp lemon zest

¼ cup lemon juice, freshly squeezed

½ red onion, finely chopped

salt and pepper to taste

⅓ cup pomegranate pips to garnish

Cook the quinoa according to the package instructions until it is 'loose and fluffy'.

While the quinoa is cooking, prep the cucumber, parsley, mint, onion and pomegranate.

Prepare the dressing by adding the oil, lemon zest and juice and salt and pepper to a jar, screw the lid on securely and shake until you have a smooth emulsion.

Once the quinoa is cooked, remove it from the heat, transfer it to your salad bowl and allow it to cool to room temperature, then add the onion, cucumber, herbs and dressing and toss through gently. Garnish with the pomegranate pips before serving.

# Tredici's Sourdough Panzanella

Serves 4–6

I consider Swellendam to be one of my hometowns. If you ever pass it on your way to the Garden Route, you should most definitely stop at Tredici (Thirteen) to enjoy a delicious plate of panzanella, and its stylish surroundings and exceptional service.

8 ripe Roma tomatoes, cut into fairly big cubes
1 tsp sea salt flakes, plus more for seasoning
1 small sourdough ciabatta loaf, cut into 4 cm cubes
3 tbsp macadamia nut oil
1 small shallot, finely grated
1 medium cloves garlic, finely grated or crushed
½ tsp Dijon mustard
3 tbsp extra-virgin olive oil
freshly ground black pepper
1 tbsp white wine vinegar or red wine vinegar
⅓ cup fresh basil, roughly chopped

Preheat the oven to 150°C.

Place the chopped tomatoes in a colander over a bowl and season them with the sea salt, stirring gently to allow the extra juice to start draining. Continue to stir gently and allow to drain for at least 15 minutes. Retain the juice.

In the meantime, in a large bowl, toss the cubed ciabatta through half the macadamia nut oil. Transfer the cubes to a baking tray and place in the oven. Bake until crisp and golden – about 15 minutes. Remove from the oven and allow to cool.

To the juice drained from the tomatoes, add the shallot, garlic, mustard, olive oil, salt, pepper and vinegar, and whisk it all together well.

Combine the toasted ciabatta, tomatoes and dressing in a large bowl. Add the basil leaves. Toss everything to coat and season with more salt and pepper. Allow it to rest for 30 minutes before serving, tossing occasionally until the dressing is completely absorbed by the bread.

# *Fennel, Apple & Walnut Slaw*

Serves 2

When looking for a quick, delicious salad to help restore your gut health, settle your tummy and accompany any meal, this should be one of your go-to recipes.

2–3 baby fennel bulbs, shredded or finely sliced

1 Granny Smith apple, grated (leave the skin on)

¼ cup walnuts, lightly toasted and roughly chopped or crushed

*Dressing*

2½ tbsp olive oil

1 tbsp raw apple cider vinegar

1 tsp honey

1 clove garlic, finely grated or crushed

salt and pepper to taste

Combine and shake together all the dressing ingredients in a jar.

Simply combine the apple and fennel in a large bowl, then add the emulsified dressing and toss it all together, finishing finally with a sprinkling of prepared walnuts.

# Cannellini Bean & Pumpkin Seed Pesto Salad

Serves 2–4

Cannellini beans are crammed full of the right kind of fibre for your friendly bacteria (microbes) to flourish; they are also high in protein and wonderfully filling. Combining them with spinach and pumpkin seed pesto makes this a densely nutritious meal.

1 (400 g) tin cannellini beans or ⅔ cup
    dried cannellini beans
1 cup baby spinach, shredded
1 small red onion, finely diced
½ cup lightly toasted pumpkin seeds
⅓ cup Kale and Pumpkin Seed Pesto
    (see page 114)

Soak the cannellini beans overnight first in plenty of filtered water and then cook them in well salted water until tender.

Drain the beans well and set aside to cool completely. Alternatively, if you are using them from a jar, drain, rinse in clean water and drain them again well in a colander before adding them to the salad bowl.

Now simply add all the other ingredients to your bowl and mix through gently, serve and enjoy.

# Broccoli & Tofu Salad

Serves 2 main portions or 4 side portions

200 g tofu

1 tbsp macadamia or coconut oil

1 tbsp brewer's yeast powder (or
   nutritional yeast flakes)

½ tsp sweet paprika

10 stems tender-stem broccoli

⅓ cup shelled edamame beans

baby lettuce leaves

salt and pepper to taste

Slice the tofu into sticks or large cubes, and then season them with the macadamia oil, brewer's yeast, paprika and salt.

Heat a cast-iron pan on high heat, transfer the marinated tofu to the hot pan and sauté until it has a lovely golden, crispy look on the outside. Transfer to a plate and allow to cool for a few minutes.

Now blanch the broccoli and edamame beans in boiling salted water for 3 minutes, drain and cool immediately.

Assemble the salad on a platter or bowl by adding the salad leaves, broccoli and edamame beans, and then the slightly cooled tofu. Dress with your choice of dressing (Blonde Pesto on page 114 works well for the recipe).

# Roasted Vegetable Salad

Serves 4 as a side dish or 2 main portions

2 small to medium aubergines
macadamia nut oil for roasting
salt to taste
2 large red peppers, quartered
    lengthways, stems and seeds
    removed
8 broccoli florets
1 cup leafy greens, washed and dried
½ cup full-fat live Greek yoghurt
2 tbsp olive oil
1 clove fresh garlic, grated or crushed
    finely
juice of half a lemon
salt and pepper to taste
sundried onions to garnish
Kale and Pumpkin Seed Pesto (see
    page 114)

Preheat the oven to 180°C.

Slice the aubergines into thin wedges, then season them well with salt and place them in a baking tray that has been generously coated with macadamia nut oil, making sure that they don't overlap.

Transfer them to the oven for 30–40 minutes, turning them over once halfway through their roasting time.

Together with the aubergine slices, in a separate baking tray, add the quartered peppers and broccoli florets and allow them a roasting time of 30–40 minutes.

While the vegetables are roasting, prepare the yoghurt sauce by mixing the yoghurt, olive oil, garlic, lemon juice, and salt and pepper.

Once the peppers and aubergines are ready, remove both from the oven to cool and then serve them on a platter along with the leafy greens, dollops of Greek yoghurt sauce, a sprinkle of sundried onions and pesto.

I am honoured to share two salad recipes from one of my favourite breakfast/lunch spots in Cape Town: The Spirit Café. Should you be near one of the Spirit Cafés (located respectively in Constantia and Gardens, Cape Town) don't miss the opportunity to drop in for a Spirit Yoga Class as well as a breakfast or lunch afterwards – you will simply float all the way home.

# The Spirit Café's Lovely Lentil Salad

Serves 8

This delicious and nutritious salad is high in protein and gut-healthy fibre, as well as being lunchbox friendly! The dressing for this recipe is exceptional and one to make in large quantities as it works well with any fresh homemade salad.

⅓ cup mix of sunflower seeds, roasted

3 cups brown lentils, cooked

2 large carrots, grated

3 courgette (zucchini), grated

1 small red cabbage, thinly sliced

¼ cup dates or cranberries

handful of spinach, thinly sliced (optional)

1 cup chopped herbs, leaves only – mint is GREAT in this

salt to taste

*Citrus dressing*

½ cup orange juice

2 tbsp lemon juice

⅓ cup olive oil

3 dates, soaked in hot water until soft)

1 tsp minced garlic

2 heaped tsp dukah (if you don't have on hand, make do with a mix of cumin and coriander seeds, and a grinding of black pepper)

pinch of chillies (optional)

1 tbsp soy sauce

Note: add a couple of teaspoons of capers (halfway through blending so the capers come out as roughly chopped … this will also depend on your salt preference)

Blend all the dressing ingredients together; let the flavours mix and meld while you prep the rest.

Prep all the ingredients for the body of the salad and toss together. Pour the dressing over and toss together.

Optional but recommended: squeeze some lemon juice over the top and add a few more twists of salt according to taste.

Toss more seeds over the top.

# The Spirit Café's Vegan Lebanese Beets

Serves 8

This is a sublime vegan twist on a classic dish, and since I love beets it's a personal favourite. It makes a great addition to any lunchbox or meal and can be made ahead and stored in the fridge quite successfully for a few days (store the dressing separately, adding it only before using).

8 medium beets, quartered
1 medium courgette, grated
1 small head of broccoli, cut into very
    small florets
½ cup frozen green peas
a pinch of chilli flakes
salt and pepper to taste
¼ cup chopped mint leaves
squeeze of lemon

*Cashew yoghurt dressing*
1 cup cashew yoghurt
2 tsp minced garlic
1 or 2 tsp date syrup (to taste)
3 tbsp tahini
1 tsp of ground cumin

Par-boil and then roast the beets in the oven at 180°C – we like to roast ours with dukah spice (use or simply sprinkle over some cumin and pink salt before roasting the beets). Once the beets are ready, allow them to cool.

Grate the courgette fine and and blanche the peas in boiling water for 3 minutes before draining them.

To make your dressing, whizz all the dressing ingredients together in a blender; let the flavours mix and meld while you prep the rest.

Add the beets to your serving bowl along with the peas, grated courgette, broccoli, chilli flakes and chopped mint; add a squeeze of lemon juice and then drizzle over the cashew and yoghurt dressing before serving.

# The Wellness Café's Coconut Chicken Salad

Serves 4

This is a delicious, fabulously fibre- and nutrient-rich salad from the wonderful Wellness Warehouse Café. As with most recipes in this chapter it is simple to prep and put together and will work exceptionally well in a lunchbox too.

2 chicken breasts, sliced into chunks

*Chicken marinade*
50 ml lemon juice
2 tbsp plain live yoghurt
1 tsp olive oil

*Salad ingredients*
1 large carrot, grated
1 small Mediterranean cucumber or large
   courgette (zucchini), grated
3 spring onions, finely sliced
⅓ cup mixed sprouts
2 heaped tbsp kimchi

*Sprinkle*
½ cup mixed, lightly toasted coconut
   shavings and sunflower seeds

*Dressing*
juice of 1 lime
3 tbsp cold pressed olive oil
salt and pepper to taste

Combine all the marinade ingredients and then allow the chicken to marinate for approximately 30 minutes to one hour, then season the pieces well with salt before transferring to a hot pan. Brown on both sides and cook through before cooling.

Prepare the dressing by simply adding all the ingredients to a jar, putting the lid on tightly and then giving it a good shake to emulsify.

Toss all the vegetables together in a bowl, then arrange the chicken pieces on top, sprinkle over the sprouts and the toasted seeds and coconut. Pour over the dressing and toss lightly before serving.

# *The Good Gut Soba Noodle Salad* *with Probiotic Peanut Miso Sauce*   Serves 4–6

Here is another delicious recipe I am pleased to share from *The Good Gut*. Authors Erica and Justin Sonnenburg say the following about this recipe: "Soba noodles are a type of Japanese noodle made from buckwheat, which, despite its name, is not a variety of wheat. Noodles made from 100 per cent wholegrain buckwheat will have the most fibre. The sauce contains miso, which is a paste made from fermented soybeans with added barley or rice. Miso is fermented using a starter that contains a species of fungus called *Aspergillus oryzae*. If you can find unpasteurised miso you will benefit not only from the fermentation products it contains but also from its living microbes (pasteurisation kills these microbes). This dish comes together easily and is perfect for a lunchbox since it is served cold or at room temperature."

250 g buckwheat noodles
½ cup edamame beans (blanched and
    shelled)
½ cup spring onions, finely sliced
¼ cup sesame seeds, lightly toasted in a
    dry pan

*Peanut miso sauce*
¼ cup sesame oil
¼ cup water
¼ cup soy sauce
4 tbsp peanut butter
2 tbsp unpasteurized miso paste (white
    or yellow)
1 tbsp brown sugar
juice of a lime

Boil the soba noodles in a medium saucepan until al dente, about 3–4 minutes. Drain noodles and cool them under running cold water.

Combine the sauce ingredients in a large mixing bowl and whisk well.

Add the cooked noodles to the mixing bowl together with the edamame beans and then toss it all well together.

Serve cold or at room temperature with the sliced spring onions and sesame seeds sprinkled over the top.

# Gut-healthy Dressings & Toppings

## Coconut Dukah

Makes 150 ml

This dukah should come with a warning … you will find yourself absentmindedly and unashamedly eating it straight from the container. It goes well with basically everything … Make lots and store it in the fridge in an airtight container.

½ cup pumpkin seeds
1 cup flaked or ⅔ cup desiccated
   coconut
⅓ cup shelled pistachios
2 tbsp nutritional yeast flakes
   (optional)

Roast the pumpkin seeds in a dry pan over medium heat, stirring frequently as these can burn or 'over-roast' very easily. As they start popping (you will hear and smell them) add the flaked coconut and stir continuously. Once the coconut starts turning golden, remove the pan from the heat and continue stirring for another minute as it cools.

Now add the shelled pistachios (note that this recipes is sans salt as the pistachios you use will most likely be salted, and will provide enough saltiness to the dukah), and the nutritional yeast flakes. Add it to your food processor or coffee grinder and whizz away until you have the crumbly consistency you crave.

# Vegan Sunflower Seed Spread/Dip

Makes 200 ml

½ cup sunflower seeds, lightly toasted in
    a dry pan
⅓ cup macadamia nut oil or cold-pressed
    olive oil
4 heaped tbsp nutritional yeast flakes
salt to taste

Simply add all the ingredients to your blender jug, then blitz until you have a creamy consistency.

# Kale and Pumpkin Seed Pesto

Makes 150 ml

1 cup roughly shredded baby kale,
    washed and dried
¼ cup olive oil
salt to taste
1 small clove garlic
juice of half a lemon
⅓ cup lightly toasted pumpkin seeds

Add all the ingredients to your food processor and pulse until you have a fairly smooth consistency.

# Blonde Pesto

Makes 150 ml

½ cup pine nuts, lightly toasted in a dry
    pan
⅓ cup cold-pressed olive oil
juice of 1 small lemon juice
1 clove garlic, grated or crushed
salt and pepper to taste

Simply add all the ingredients to your blender jug, then blitz until you have a creamy yet still slightly course consistency.

# The Good Gut's Parsley Almond Pesto

Makes 150 ml

A delicious and very nutritious recipe from Justin & Erica Sonnenburg's book, *The Good Gut*

2 cups fresh parsley
2 cloves garlic
½ cup unsalted almonds (soak them
    overnight, drain and then lightly roast
    to add flavour and crunch)
2–3 tbsp extra-virgin olive oil
1–2 tbsp lemon juice
salt to taste

Add all the ingredients to a food processor and blend until smooth.

# Apple Cider Vinegar Gut-healing Dressing

Makes ½ cup

¼ cup cold-pressed flaxseed or avocado
    oil
3 tbsp of raw (and cloudy) apple cider
    vinegar
1 tbsp raw honey
salt and pepper to taste

Simply add all the ingredients to a jar, secure the lid tightly and shake until you have a smooth emulsion.

# Holy Guacamole

Makes ½ cup

2 ripe avocadoes, peeled and halved
1 tbsp of cold pressed olive oil
juice of 1 lemon
1 clove garlic, finely grated (optional)
salt to taste

Mash all the ingredients together in a deep mixing bowl. I like using my whisk to mash avocadoes – so much easier than using a fork.

# Prebiotic Plant-based Meals

## Fibre-rich vegetarian and vegan recipes

### INTRODUCTION

The secret to good gut health is to include a large variety of vegetables (and plenty of them) to your daily diet. Try to make a shift towards a more plant-based diet, going meatless for a few days a week.

In this chapter you will find some fabulously fibre-rich plant-based meals to satisfy your taste buds and your microbes that are all easy to prepare, tasty and satisfying. You can also find some more yummy plant-based recipes in my first book *The Yoga Kitchen*.

# Massaman Curry

This is an exceptionally tasty, low-effort recipe to include a wide variety of vegetables to your day; serving it with quinoa adds extra texture and sufficient protein.

3 large carrots, scrubbed and cut into
   1-cm-thick medallions
3 red onions, sliced lengthways
1 thumb-sized piece fresh ginger, peeled
   and finely grated
1 clove garlic, finely grated
2 red peppers, cut into large chunks
1 head broccoli, cut into florets
1 head cauliflower, cut into florets
1 cup green beans, topped and tailed,
   then halved
4 tbsp Massaman curry paste
1 heaped tsp turmeric
salt and pepper to taste
1 (400 ml) tin coconut cream

Sauté the carrots, onions, garlic and ginger in a deep saucepan or pot for 15 minutes on low heat, stirring frequently.

Add all the other vegetables as well as the curry paste and turmeric and season well with salt. Stir through until the veggies are coated with the curry paste, then add the coconut cream and stir through gently before placing the lid on the pan/pot. Allow the curry to gently simmer for a further 10–15 minutes before serving with fluffy quinoa.

# Vegetarian Biryani

2 tbsp coconut oil

2 green cardamom pods

2 cinnamon sticks, about 1 inch each

2 cloves

1 tbsp cumin seeds

1 tbsp ginger, grated

1 tbsp garlic, grated

1 medium cauliflower, separated into florets

1 heaped tsp mild curry paste or ground masala

½ cup coriander leaves, chopped

½ cup mint leaves, chopped

1 cup Greek yoghurt or coconut yoghurt, strained

salt to taste

3 cups of well-cooked brown basmati rice, soaked prior to cooking for a couple of hours for additional digestive benefits

½ cup cashew nuts, chopped

⅓ cup sundried onion flakes to garnish

Preheat the oven to 180°C.

Heat the oil in a deep cast-iron pan. When hot, add the cardamom pods, cinnamon sticks and cloves to it and sauté for 30 seconds on medium heat. Add the cumin seeds, ginger, garlic and cauliflower florets, and sauté for about 5 minutes, stirring frequently.

Add the mild masala or curry paste, coriander and mint leaves and the yoghurt. Mix well and allow the cauliflower to cook until almost tender, add salt to taste and then take it off the heat.

In an ovenproof dish, pour out half the cooked rice and then on top of the rice add a layer of the vegetable/yoghurt mixture, add another layer of cooked rice before adding the remaining veggie mixture. Transfer the dish to the oven for 15 minutes.

Before serving, sprinkle a generous amount of crushed cashews and sundried onion flakes over the top.

# Middle Eastern Butternut Stew

Serves 4–6

Butternut squash delivers an ample dose of fibre for your friendly microbes to feast on, making it an exceptionally good gut-health choice. It provides significant amounts of potassium, important for bone health, and vitamin B6, essential for the proper functioning of both the nervous and immune systems.

1 large onion, finely chopped

2 tbsp coconut oil

4 cloves garlic, freshly crushed or finely grated

1 pinch of cayenne pepper (optional)

1 tsp ground cumin

1 tsp coriander

5 Roma tomatoes, chopped

1 small butternut, chopped into small cubes

1 large carrot, finely chopped

2 cups vegetable stock, or chicken/beef bone broth

salt and pepper to taste

toasted sesame and nigella seeds to garnish (optional)

Fry the onion in half the coconut oil until it is soft and turning golden, then add garlic and all the dry spices and sauté, stirring well, for a further 2 minutes.

Add the chopped tomatoes and sauté for another 5 minutes, stirring frequently.

Add the butternut, carrot and stock, season with salt and pepper, stir through once, and then place the lid on the pot and turn the heat down to low, allowing the stew to simmer for 40 minutes.

Serve with cooked quinoa and a sprinkling of toasted seeds of your choice.

# Winter Retreat Chilli

Serves 4–6

This recipe is always a favourite during my winter retreats. I guarantee your family will eat it (even if they aren't bean lovers or plant-based food fans) and you will love it too, especially since it's so easy to throw together. On a nutritional note this dish is packed with fibre for your microbes, serving it with corn chips is optional, but makes a great substitute for rice or couscous as well as adding an additional punch of fibre and fun.

1 tbsp coconut oil

3 yellow/brown onions, finely chopped

2 medium tomatoes, finely chopped

2 heaped tsp ground cumin

1 tsp ground coriander

1 heaped tsp dried oregano

1 heaped tsp sweet paprika

2–3 cloves garlic, finely grated or crushed

2 tbsp tomato paste

½ tsp brown sugar

1 (400 g) tin baked beans

1 cup frozen corn

100 ml water

black pepper & cayenne pepper to taste

*To serve*

½ cup Greek yoghurt (or more should you prefer)

1–2 avocadoes, diced or made into guacamole (see page 115)

2–4 spring onions, finely chopped

corn chips

Sauté the chopped onions over low heat. They should be golden and sweet before you add the garlic. After another 2 minutes add the finely chopped tomatoes. Sauté this mixture until the tomatoes start to disintegrate and form a thick red sauce.

Next add the spices, oregano, tomato paste, sugar, and salt and pepper to taste and give it a good stir. Then add the beans, corn and water.

Allow the mixture to simmer over low heat for 25 minutes before serving in bowls, garnishing each bowl with a dollop of Greek yoghurt and avocado, finely sliced spring onions and corn chips.

# New Age-y Lasagne

Serves 4–6

3 cups butternut, cubed

150 g brown mushrooms, coarsely
grated

2 cups shredded baby spinach

1 tsp oregano

1 tsp sweet basil

3 cloves garlic, finely grated

2 cups tomato passata

approximately 12 sheets of lasagne
sheets made from pulses

white/cheese sauce (see page 137)

salt to taste

Preheat the oven to 170°C.

Steam the butternut until tender, drain and set aside.

In a deep saucepan sauté the grated mushrooms until they are almost cooked through and then add the herbs, garlic and spinach. Sauté for a further 2 minutes before adding the passata, then allow to simmer for a few more minutes until the spinach is wilted and the sauce has reduced a little.

In an ovenproof dish, add a thin layer of tomato mixture, then place the first layer of lasagne sheets, then a layer of butternut, and then more tomato mixture on top of the butternut. Continue layering until all your ingredients have been used up. Finish by adding a thick layer of white sauce on top.

Bake for 35–40 minutes. Allow to cool and settle slightly before serving.

Note: To turn your white sauce into a delicious cheese sauce, grate some pecorino cheese into the hot white sauce, then stir through well until the cheese is melted.

# Sweetcorn Fritters

Serves 4

Sweetcorn is a great prebiotic food, which helps good bacteria to thrive. This recipe also contains chickpea flour, which is a good source of plant-based protein, and is gluten free.

The antioxidant activity, which helps protect your body from cancer and heart disease, is actually increased when sweetcorn is cooked. Sweetcorn is loaded with lutein and zeaxanthin, two phytochemicals that promote healthy vision.

1½ cups frozen sweetcorn
½ cup chickpea flour
1 small red onion, finely diced
1 tsp coriander
½ tsp fine salt
⅓ cup water
2–3 tsp coconut oil for shallow frying

Add all the ingredients, except the oil, to a large mixing bowl and stir.

Heat a heavy-based non-stick pan with a teaspoon of coconut oil for each batch of fritters.

Using your hand (clean, obviously), form the fritter mixture into snooker-ball-sized rounds and then gently transfer them to the hot pan in batches of 3 or 4. Carefully press down on them to flatten slightly (they should be about 2 cm thick) and allow them to shallow fry on medium heat until the one side has a lovely rich golden colour; turn each fritter carefully and fry on the other side.

Once you have made all the fritters you can serve them with a salad, or simply some diced avocado and plain full-fat yoghurt seasoned with salt and pepper. They can be eaten hot or cold.

# *Prebiotic Bobotie*

Serves 6–8

¾ cup brown lentils, soaked overnight

3 large jewel (orange flesh) sweet potato, peeled and cut into large chunks

3 slices of wholewheat sourdough bread, crusts removed

1 (400 g) tin coconut milk

2 onions, chopped

2 eggs, beaten

3 tbsp coconut oil or ghee

2 tsp garam masala

1 tsp turmeric

1 heaped tsp ground coriander

1 heaped tsp cumin

2 tsp brown sugar

5 cloves garlic

1 tbsp ginger, grated

salt and pepper to taste

3 eggs

5 bay leaves

Preheat the oven to 180°C.

Drain the soaked lentils and cook them in well salted water until tender. Drain well and set aside.

While the lentils are cooking, place the cubed sweet potato in a baking tray (greased with a little coconut oil) and roast for 30 minutes; they will continue cooking later when the dish is transferred to the oven for the final cooking stage.

In a shallow, wide bowl, add the bread and the coconut milk to soak, and set aside.

Next, in a deep cast-iron pan, fry the onions until soft in ghee or coconut oil, then add all the spices (except for the bay leaves), garlic and ginger, and continue sautéing for a further 3 minutes. Add the cooked and drained lentils as well as the roasted sweet potato, along with the sugar.

Remove the soaked bread from the coconut milk, squeezing out most of the liquid, and retaining the coconut milk for later use. Add the soaked bread to the lentil/sweet potato mixture, mashing it with a fork and mixing it well with the lentil mixture. Season with black pepper and salt and stir through well.

Transfer the lentil mixture to an ovenproof dish, beat the eggs and coconut milk together (seasoning it with more salt), then pour this 'custard' over the top of the lentil filling and decorate the top with the bay leaves. Turn the oven down to 150°C and bake for 45 minutes.

Serve with mango chutney, sliced banana and lightly toasted desiccated coconut.

# Bombay Lentil, Potato & Egg Curry

Serves 4

This curry is a great dish to prepare in winter. It delivers lots of beneficial fibre for your microbes and is rich in protein.

1 tbsp ghee or coconut oil

1 tsp black mustard seeds

2 onions, 1 chopped, and 1 quartered

2 green chillies, 1 finely sliced and 1 halved

2 cloves garlic, finely grated or freshly crushed

½ cup fresh coriander, leaves and stalks separated

2 tsp turmeric or garam masala or ground cumin

1 tsp ground fennel

1 tbsp vegetable stock powder

2 medium potatoes, peeled and cut into 2.5 cm cubes

3 eggs, boiled

½ cup brown lentils, cooked in well salted water until tender, but not broken

2 tbsp tomato paste

1 tsp brown sugar

1 lemon, juiced

Heat the oil in a large sauce pan or casserole dish, and splutter the mustard seeds till they pop. Add the onions and sauté until soft and golden.

Using your food processor, whizz the quartered onion, halved chilli, garlic and coriander stalks with ¼ teaspoon salt to a paste – with a splash of water if needed.

Once the onions are soft, stir in the onion paste and spices and fry for 4–5 minutes until fragrant. Add the stock powder with one cup of water and bring to a simmer. Add the potatoes, cover with a lid and simmer for 10 minutes.

While the potatoes are cooking, boil the eggs and then place them in cold water before peeling them. Once peeled, quarter them lengthways.

Now add the cooked and drained lentils, tomato paste, sugar and half the lemon juice to the potato mixture, stirring it through gently.

Take the lid off the curry and allow it to continue simmering for 10–15 minutes until the potatoes are tender and the gravy reduces and thickens.

Taste the curry and season with more salt, black pepper and lemon juice if needed. Add the eggs to the top, then turn off the heat and place the lid back on so the eggs warm up for a minute or so.

Serve with sliced green chillies, a squeeze of fresh lemon juice and chopped coriander leaves.

# La Cuccina Sweet Potato, Mushroom & Nut Curry

Serves 4–6

This sublime gut-friendly vegan curry recipe is from the lovely La Cuccina in Hout Bay. The food at La Cuccina is incredible and they really have some great gut-healthy options in their breakfast and lunch buffets. My only problem is that I find it virtually impossible to decide what to have. They have plenty of dairy- and wheat-free options, but I highly recommend their Chocolate & Almond Loaf which is pretty much heaven on a plate, and (obviously) made from almond flour instead of wheat flour.

1 tbsp of coconut oil

1 yellow/brown onion, finely chopped

2 cloves of garlic, finely grated or crushed

1 small punnet of button mushrooms, quartered

3 large sweet potatoes, peeled and cubed

400 g can coconut milk

1 cup vegetable stock

1 tablespoon curry powder

½ cup air-roasted cashew nuts

In a large, deep saucepan start by sautéing the onions on low heat in the coconut oil until they are becoming golden and fragrant, stirring frequently,

Add the grated garlic and mushrooms and sauté for a further 10 minutes, stirring frequently, then take the pan of the heat and set aside.

In a separate pan, start sautéing the cubed sweet potato on low heat until the cubes are cooked through, then add them to the saucepan with the mushrooms and return it to the hob on low heat.

Next add coconut milk, vegetable stock and curry powder. Cook at low heat for a further 10 minutes

Before serving, sprinkle over the air-roasted cashew nuts to complete the dish. Best served with brown basmati rice.

# Simple Egg Fried Rice

Serves 4–6

6 stalks spring onions

3 cloves garlic, finely grated or
   crushed

3 tbsp sesame oil

1 tsp coconut oil

1 heaped tbsp unpasteurised miso
   paste

1½ cups cooked brown basmati rice

2 eggs

½ cup edamame beans

salt to taste

juice of 1 small lime

tamari sauce

In a hot cast-iron pan, add the sliced spring onions and garlic together with the sesame oil, coconut oil and miso paste and flash-fry the onions in this mixture. Next add the rice and raw eggs, edamame beans, season well with salt and over high heat stir-fry through until the eggs are cooked. Season with salt.

Serve with a squeeze of lime juice, a drizzle of sesame oil and tamari sauce.

# Gut-healthy Sauces & Sides

A good sauce or side dish can make a run-of-the-mill meal spectacular. The recipes included here are meant to replace traditional favourites with gut-healthy ingredients.

## White/Cheese Sauce

2 heaped tbsp ghee

1–2 heaped tbsp chickpea flour to thicken the sauce (the more you add the thicker the sauce)

2 cups A2 milk

¼ cup pecorino cheese (omit for a plain white/béchamel sauce)

salt to taste

Start by simply adding the ghee and chickpea flour in a saucepan, mixing the two together well as the ghee starts warming on low heat.

Then add the A2 milk, and whisk well initially, then stir slowly as the milk heats and the sauce starts to thicken.

Once you have a sufficiently thick sauce, take the saucepan off the heat, allow to cool for 5 minutes, and then stir in the grated pecorino and season with salt.

## Pea & Asparagus Pilaf with Blonde Pesto

1 cup brown basmati rice

2½ cups vegetable stock or chicken bone broth

½ cup frozen peas

½ cup fine asparagus, woody part removed, but that part is a super-prebiotic

½ cup Blonde Pesto (see page 114)

salt and pepper to taste

Start by soaking the brown basmati rice for a couple of hours, then drain it well and add it to a stock pot or deep saucepan along with the stock or broth and salt. Bring it to the boil and reduce the heat to a simmer for 30 minutes, cooking with the lid on.

Once the rice is fully cooked, turn the heat off but leave it to keep steaming in the pot with the lid on.

Blanche the peas and asparagus for 3 minutes in well-salted boiling water. Remove them immediately from the water to drain and add them to the rice, stir through lightly. Dress generously with Blonde Pesto and lots of freshly ground pepper.

# Jewel Sweet Potato Mash

6 large jewel (orange flesh) sweet
  potato
2 tbsp ghee
1 tbsp olive oil
salt to taste

Start by peeling and then halving the sweet potatoes. Boil them until tender in well-salted water, retaining a little cooking water when draining them, before mashing them together with the ghee, olive oil and some more sea salt.

# Sweet Potato Fries

3-4 large jewel (orange flesh) sweet
  potato
salt to taste
2 heaped tbsp of coconut oil

Preheat the oven to 180°C.

Start by peeling the sweet potatoes and then cutting them into 'chips'. Season them with salt, then transfer them to a shallow baking tin. Add the warmed coconut oil before giving them a good shake so that all the sweet potato pieces are covered with a thin layer of oil.

Pop them in the oven for 45 minutes, giving them another shake halfway through.

# Sesame Miso Broccoli

300 g tender-stem broccoli
1 tbsp sesame oil
1 tsp miso paste
salt to taste
2 tbsp toasted sesame seeds

Blanche the tender-stem broccoli in boiling water for about 3 minutes. You want to retain the crunch and colour. Drain immediately and toss through the sesame oil, miso paste and salt. Finish by sprinkling over lightly toasted sesame seeds before serving.

Note: Toast the seeds in a dry pan over medium heat for about 3 minutes, stirring continuously until they are golden, then allow to cool completely before using them.

# Conscious Flexitarian

## Animal protein gut-friendly meals

### INTRODUCTION

Protein deficiency seems to be a very real fear in western society, but with a well-balanced, mostly plant-based diet, this is very unlikely.

Eating too much animal protein can put a strain on our kidneys and allows undesirable second-hand antibiotics and growth hormones into our diet.

When it comes to meat I am very picky about the source of the meat. Often I get told that buying organic, grass-fed meat is simply too expensive, but my simple solution to this budget-bending conundrum is to replace half of your meals with plant-based proteins. That way you are freeing up some extra funds to buy good quality pasture-fed and antibiotic-free meat, as well as adding the essential fibre to your diet that your microbes love. For good meat alternative meals navigate to the chapter Prebiotic Plant-based Meals.

With that being said, in this chapter, Conscious Flexitarian, I have included some easy and delicious gut-friendly recipes that include meat or fish.

# Miso Sesame Chicken

Serves 4

This is a crowd pleaser and a timesaver. In addition it's very gut friendly and even fussy offspring will eat it with enthusiasm.

2 cups brown basmati rice

2 skinless chicken breasts, cut into strips

1 cup tender-stem broccoli

1 tbsp coconut oil

10 spring onions, chopped

1 tbsp rice vinegar

2 tsp miso paste

1 tsp grated ginger

1 tsp grated garlic

1 tbsp toasted sesame seeds

Soak the basmati rice for approximately 2 hours, then drain and cook for at least 30 minutes in well-salted water until fluffy.

Season the raw chicken with salt.

Steam the tender-stem broccoli gently and set aside.

Heat the coconut oil in a deep pan and sauté the spring onions and chicken pieces (on fairly high heat) until the chicken is cooked through but still tender. Add the rice vinegar, miso paste, grated ginger and garlic and steamed broccoli, and continue stir-frying for 2 minutes on high heat.

Lastly, stir in the cooked basmati rice until the whole mixture is coated in the sauce.

Serve with a sprinkle of lightly toasted sesame seeds.

# Moussaka

If you're after a low-carb, fibre-filled supper this is it! It's not only tasty and filling, it also cooks and freezes well, so when making this consider doubling the recipe.

This dish is somewhat lengthy to prepare but not complicated, and entirely worth it once the first glorious mouthful has been enjoyed. It's low-carb and full of vegetable fibre, which equals valuable food for your microbes.

2 large aubergines sliced thinly into discs (about 1 cm in thickness)

macadamia oil for roasting

salt and pepper to taste

1 tbsp coconut oil or ghee

2 brown/yellow onions, finely diced

400 g ground beef or lamb

150 g Portobello mushrooms, de-stemmed and grated

1–2 cloves garlic, finely grated

2 heaped tbsp tomato puree

3 cups baby leaf spinach, tightly packed and shredded

250 g jar additive-free tomato passata

1 tsp dried oregano

1 tsp ground cinnamon

3 bay leaves

1 heaped tsp sweet paprika

½ tsp brown sugar

¼ cup pecorino cheese

¼ cup goat's cheese feta

1 tbsp fresh parsley, finely chopped

*Aubergine prep:* Preheat the oven to 150°C. Grease a baking tray (you may need 2) generously with some macadamia nut oil and then arrange the sliced aubergine in single layers on it. Season them with salt before placing them in the oven for 40 minutes, checking on them every 10 minutes or so to turn them over when needed to allow both sides to crisp up. Remove from the oven and cool for a couple of minutes.

*Tomato-meat sauce prep:* In some ghee or coconut oil, sauté the onions until soft and golden, then add the ground beef or lamb and continue stirring, separating the ground meat and sautéing until the meat is browned and crumbly. Add the mushrooms and continue sautéing for another 10 minutes.

Next add the garlic and spinach, sauté for another 5 minutes before adding the tomato puree, as well as all the spices and herbs (except the parsley), half a teaspoon of sugar to regulate the acidity as well as salt and pepper to taste. Turn down the heat and allow this mixture to simmer for 15 minutes without a lid on.

*Final prep:* Turn the oven up to 180°C. In a large ovenproof dish add a 2 cm thick layer of tomato/meat sauce, then a single, slightly overlapping layer of cooked aubergine, and continue this layering process until both the sauce and aubergines are used up. It doesn't really matter which layer ends up on the top, but a thin layer of tomato mixture is preferable.

Sprinkle the pecorino cheese in an even layer over the top and pop the dish into the oven for 20 minutes.

When the 20 minutes are up, remove the dish from the oven and crumble the feta and a sprinkle of fresh parsley over the top and serve.

# Mike's Oxtail with Sweet Potato Mash

Serves 6–8

My father-in-law makes the most delicious oxtail; it really goes down well with all ages, making it a fabulous winter family-friendly Sunday lunch. This oxtail stew is full of gut-health benefits such as an abundance of gelatine and plenty of fibre from the added vegetables. Oxtail has a lengthy cooking time to ensure tenderness, but the preparation time is minimal, so start early and then sit back and enjoy the marvellous fragrance wafting from the kitchen.

3 onions, chopped
1 kg oxtail pieces
salt and pepper to taste
2 (400 g) tins chopped tomatoes
300 ml dry white wine
8 leeks, sliced
8 carrots, cubed
1–2 sprigs rosemary
3 cloves garlic

Preheat the oven to 180°C.

Evenly pack the onions and oxtail pieces, seasoned with salt, in a large baking tray coated with a little ghee, and then transfer it to thethe oven for 30 minutes to brown and seal the meat.

Remove the baking tray from the oven and add all the other ingredients, including the white wine, mixing it all well for even flavour distribution. Season well with salt and black pepper and seal the dish with aluminium foil. Turn the oven down to 160°C and return to the oven for a further 3 hours.

Approximately 30 minutes before the oxtail is ready, you can prepare some glorious sweet potato mash to go with it (see page 139).

# Chicken, Leek & Cannellini Bean Stew

Serves 4–6

Cannellini beans and leeks are gut-health rock stars. This stew is incredibly simple to throw together and the perfect winter evening meal.

2 onions, finely chopped

2 tbsp ghee/coconut oil

6–8 baby leeks, roughly chopped

3 carrots, finely sliced or chopped

4 cloves garlic, finely crushed or grated

4–6 boneless, skinless chicken thighs, trimmed and cut into chunks

salt to taste

1.2 cups vegetable or bone broth

juice of 1 small lemon

2 cups baby spinach, washed and dried

1 (400 g) tin cannellini beans

black pepper

olive oil

Fry the onions in some ghee or coconut oil until they are golden and beginning to caramelise (it will need at least 30 minutes on low heat with a stir every now and again).

Add the leeks and carrots and sauté for a further 5 minutes before adding the garlic and chicken pieces. Season with salt and then turn the heat up to high and sauté the chicken and vegetable mix until the chicken turns golden.

Lastly add the broth/stock, lemon juice, spinach and well drained cannellini beans, stirring it all together gently and allowing it to simmer over low heat for a further 15 minutes without the lid on.

Serve with a good grinding of black pepper and a drizzle of olive oil.

# Probiotic Burger & Sweet Potato Fries

Serves 4

3 large jewel (orange flesh) sweet
  potato
drizzle of coconut oil for frying
1 cup guacamole (see page 115)
1 cup leafy greens or any lettuce of your
  choice
400 g ground beef
½ cup Golden Sauerkraut (see page 87 or
  use store bought live sauerkraut)
salt and pepper to taste

Preheat the oven to 180°C.

Peel and slice the sweet potato into fries and then spread them onto a baking tray with a drizzle of coconut oil (shaking them well to distribute the oil over the fries evenly). Transfer them to the oven to roast for approximate 20–30 minutes.

Wash and dry the leafy greens or lettuce.

Divide the ground beef into 4 balls, and then press down on the balls to form patties. Season well with salt.

Next place the patties in a pre-heated (on high heat) cast-iron or non-stick pan (Teflon free). They will need approximately 4 minutes on each side, only turning them over once; the less they're handled the better.

Now assemble the 'burgers' by plating them with the salad leaf layer first, then the patties, next the guacomole, and lastly the sauerkraut. Add a side of sweet potato fries.

Serve immediately and enjoy.

# Lamb & Aubergine Tagine

Serves 4

Although this is a lengthy dish to make cooking-time wise, it really makes up for it in its simplicity and little prep-work. Another great idea is to pop it in your slow cooker (after sautéing the onions first in a pan, just add the whole shebang to the slow cooker pot) and allow it to cook slowly for 3 hours.

4 medium yellow/brown onions

1 tbsp of ghee

8 lamb knuckle pieces

3 cloves garlic

3 tsp ground coriander seeds

2 tsp ground cumin

1 tsp sweet paprika

½ tsp sumac

salt and pepper to taste

2 medium aubergines

½ cup water

400 g jar tomato passata

1 tbsp tomato puree

½ cup full fat Greek yoghurt

1 cup chickpeas, cooked and well
　drained

Sauté the onions in ghee for at least 20 minutes over low heat until they start turning golden (longer if you have the patience for it).

Then add the knuckles, garlic, spices and salt, and brown the meat for about 15 minutes on medium heat, turning them as needed.

Add the aubergines to the pot, then add the water and turn to low heat and allow to simmer for 50 minutes with the lid on.

After 40 minutes of cooking time, add the pasta sauce, tomato puree, yoghurt and chickpeas, and simmer for a further 20 minutes with the lid off, stirring through gently once or twice during that time.

Serve it on some pre-soaked, well-cooked brown basmati rice, or quinoa for a low-carb option.

# Hot Smoked Mackerel Carbonara

Serves 4

Everybody adores carbonara pasta. This is my gut-friendly version that offers plenty of fibre from the pulse pasta. The pecorino cheese and mackerel (or salmon) are all rich in Omega 3s which research has shown improves leaky gut. Omega 3 is also important for cardiovascular health, healthy skin and to fight inflammation.

2 fillets hot-smoked mackerel (or salmon) skin removed, de-boned and flaked

2 tbsp ghee

4 leeks, finely diced

2 cloves garlic, finely grated

2 large eggs, yolks separated (you can keep the whites in the fridge for baking)

200 ml cream

¼ cup pecorino cheese, finely grated

salt to taste

1 tsp freshly ground black pepper

1 packet of pulse spaghetti pasta

Start by removing the skin of the fish as well as any bones and excess fat, then flake it and set aside.

In the ghee, sauté the diced leeks on low heat until they start becoming soft and fragrant – they will need approximately 15 minutes.

Add the grated garlic and continue sautéing for another 2 minutes on low heat. Remove and set aside.

Next, separate the yolks from the eggs, and then beat them together with the cream. Return pan to the heat and add the egg and cream custard, seasoning well with salt and black pepper. Stir continuously until it starts thickening.

Once the sauce has thickened, take it off the heat, allow to cool for 2 minutes and then stir in the finely grated pecorino cheese until it has fully melted into the sauce. Set the sauce aside with a lid on the pot.

Cook the pulse pasta as per the package instructions in salted water, then drain well and return to its cooking pot. Add the carbonara sauce and stir it through the hot cooked pasta.

Serve the pasta plated and add a portion of flaked fish to each plate along with a grinding of black pepper.

# Glorious Oven-roasted Cabbage & Bacon

Serves 4 main portions
or 8 starter portions

Cabbage is such an underrated vegetable. Not only is it a fabulously microbe friendly and nutrition-rich vegetable, but is also wonderfully delicious when roasted. Make sure you choose pasture-fed naturally smoked bacon; it is an exceptionally good source of Omega 3.

1 tbsp ghee

1 medium white cabbage, cut lengthways into 8 wedges

macadamia oil for roasting

⅓ cup pine nuts

16 strips smoked streaky bacon

Blonde Pesto (see page 114)

salt and pepper to taste

Preheat the oven to 160°C.

Coat the base of a large roasting pan with a thin layer of ghee and place the quartered cabbage in it, season with salt, drizzle with macadamia nut oil, then transfer to the oven (with the fan on preferably) for 30 minutes.

While the cabbage pieces are roasting, toast the pine nuts lightly in a dry pan over medium heat on the hob until they turn golden, stirring frequently. Remove them from the heat and transfer to a bowl to cool.

Remove the half-roasted cabbage, keeping the oven on, and lay 2 strips of bacon over each piece. Return them to the oven for a further 25 minutes.

When the cabbage and bacon emerges from the oven in all its fragrant glory, simply drizzle over the Blonde Pesto, sprinkle with pine nuts and season with flaky sea salt and freshly ground pepper before serving.

# Gutsy Chimichurri Chicken Skewers

Serves 4

These skewers are always a big hit in our house. To increase the fibre content you can add other veggies such as Brussels sprouts (delicious when roasted) as well as peppers.

4 chicken thighs, deboned and skin removed, cut into large chunks

4 tbsp chimichurri paste/sauce

salt to taste

4 medium courgettes (zucchini), cut into 2½ cm long pieces

2 medium red onions, peeled and quartered

4–8 large bamboo skewers

Add the chicken pieces and chimichurri sauce to a bowl, season well with salt and stir through to make sure all the pieces are equally covered with the sauce. Set aside and allow to marinate for 20 minutes or more if possible.

Turn the oven on to 180°C.

Once the chicken has marinated for 20 minutes or more, skewer the chicken and vegetables in layers onto bamboo skewers, then place them on a baking tray and transfer to the oven to bake for 40 minutes.

Once the skewers are cooked serve them with an additional drizzle of chimichurri sauce should you wish, a salad of your choice and some quinoa or roasted sweet potatoes.

# The Good Gut's Sesame Seed-crusted Salmon

## with Green Beans and Orange Miso Sauce

Serves 4

This recipe, generously shared by the authors of *The Good Gut*, Erica and Justin Sonnenburg, is truly delicious. Here is Erica's and Justin's introduction to it: "Seeds are a wonderful source of dietary fibre, healthy oils, protein and various micronutrients. We keep a variety of seeds in our pantry to sprinkle on salads, cooked vegetables, hot cereal and even yoghurt. This is an easy recipe to pull together on a weeknight but is also sophisticated enough for a dinner party."

½ cup sesame seeds, hulled

4 fillets wild salmon

2 tbsp olive oil

400 g green beans, washed and ends trimmed

1 tbsp orange zest

1 tbsp sesame oil

salt and pepper to taste

*Orange miso sauce*

1 cup orange juice

2 tbsp unpasteurized miso paste (white or yellow)

1 tbsp sesame oil

1 tbsp ginger, grated

1 tbsp orange zest

Spread the sesame seeds on a large plate and press the salmon fillets onto the seeds to coat.

Heat 1 tablespoon of olive oil over medium heat in a large skillet. Add the salmon and cook for approximately 4 minutes on each side until cooked through completely. Remove the fillets from the skillet and cover with foil to keep them warm.

Coat the skillet with the remaining olive oil and add the green beans, orange zest and a seasoning of salt. Sauté on medium heat until the green beans are cooked but still crisp, about 5 minutes. Season with salt and pepper.

*For the sauce:* blend all the sauce ingredients together. Serve the salmon and green beans with a generous drizzle of the sauce.

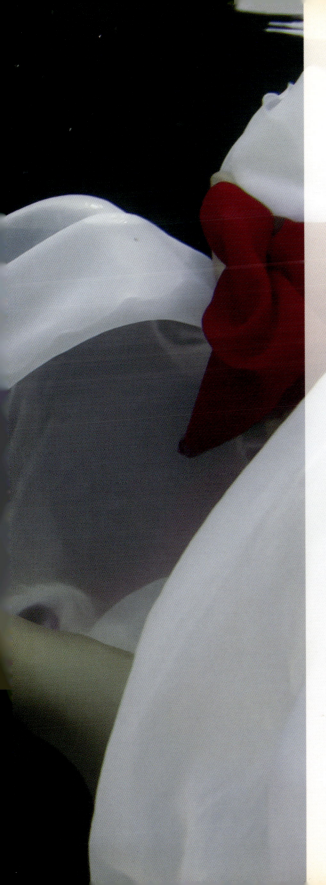

# Sensible Sweets

## Gut-healthy treats and pudding

### INTRODUCTION

Life without a little sweetness would be utterly depressing.

My philosophy is that our bodies can cope with a little sugar (and I obviously exclude those suffering with diabetes in this statement) as long as we choose an overall active and healthy lifestyle.

When a diet is crammed full of sugary drinks, refined white flours, etc., then we certainly shouldn't include puddings as well, but if your day has been filled with good fibre-rich wholefoods, you can allow yourself one well-chosen sweet treat every now and again.

You will find though that the less sugar you eat, the less you crave it, and by making the shift to only fibre-rich wholefoods, your sugar cravings will disappear.

# Rooibos & Lemon Jelly

Serves 4–6

If you are looking for a truly healing dessert, jellies really tick all the boxes. Gelatine is 30% glycine, which has been shown to improve gut health by repairing the intestinal wall and sealing the gut lining – which is essential for healing leaky gut syndrome and the auto-immune conditions that stem from leaky gut, such as rheumatoid arthritis and allergies. Combining gelatine with anti-oxidant rich rooibos tea is one of those smug food moments.

2 cups green rooibos, strongly brewed in a deep saucepan over high heat for about 10 minutes
1 heaped tsp gelatine, pre-soaked in ½ cup filtered water
2–3 heaped tbsp brown sugar
juice of 1 lemon

Add the gelatine mixture and sugar to the piping hot tea, then stir continuously until all the gelatine grains are fully dissolved. Add the lemon juice and continue stirring for another minute or so.

Cover the bowl and place it in the fridge for 2–3 hours to set.

# The Good Gut's Mango Lassi Bowl

Serves 2

I've always loved mango lassis. This recipe is from *The Good Gut* by Justin and Erica Sonnenburg; I have adjusted it slightly by making it into a smoothie bowl.

2½ cups homemade yoghurt (see page 88)

2 cups frozen or fresh mango chunks

1 tsp ground cardamom

1 tsp chopped fresh mint

1 tbsp honey

granadilla/passion fruit to garnish (optional)

seeds to garnish (optional)

Combine the yoghurt, mango, cardamom, mint and honey in a blender and blitz until smooth.

Decorate with some passion fruit (granadilla), mint leaves and seeds before serving.

# Apple Stew Crumble

Serves 4

6 Granny Smith cooking apples

½ cup water

1 tbsp ghee

salt to taste

2 tbsp raw honey/maple syrup

2 tsp ground cinnamon

¾ cup mixed cashews and walnuts,
   lightly toasted in a dry pan and then
   crumbled

Peel and core the apples and then cube them into small evenly sized pieces.

Add the apples, water, ghee, salt, honey/syrup and cinnamon in a heavy-bottomed pan and cook for about 25 minutes on medium heat, stirring regularly.

Transfer the stewed apples to a wide dish and sprinkle with the crumbled nuts before serving.

# Raspberry & Yoghurt Mousse

Serves 2

1 heaped tsp gelatine
½ cup boiling water
1 cup homemade yoghurt (see page 88)
⅓ cup pulped, fresh raspberries

Dissolve the gelatine completely in the boiling water. Once dissolved, combine all the ingredients in a bowl.

Using a hand blender, blend all the combined ingredients together, transfer it to your serving dish/bowl, cover with cling film or a lid and store in the fridge for 2–3 hours to set.

Note: Add a few drops of stevia or a tbsp of brown sugar to the gelatine and boiling water should you wish for it to be a bit sweeter.

# Blondies

This delicious treat is free from refined sugars, grains and flours. In addition it is very high in fibre and good fats, and will satisfy a sweet craving successfully.

My first book, *The Yoga Kitchen*, has a recipe for vegan, grain-free, no-bake brownies (what a mouthful) and whenever I have served them at one of my retreats a book was immediately sold. They are just that good.

Here is its sister recipe which I sometimes make when there's no dark chocolate in the house. They're great for lunchboxes or for a breakfast on the run.

1 cup macadamia or cashew butter
1 cup pitted dates
½ cup desiccated coconut
3 tbsp peanut butter (can be substituted with some more macadamia or cashew butter)
1 tsp ground cinnamon
½ tsp sea salt

Simply add all the ingredients to your food processor jug and pulse until you have a smooth mixture, then spoon it into a rectangular or square Pyrex dish lined with cling wrap, smoothing it out and pressing it down into an equally thick layer.

Cover it with cling film and pop it into the freezer for 30 minutes. Remove and slice it into squares to be stored in an airtight container in the fridge. They should last for at week.

# Chocolate Pots

This is a fairly guilt-free dessert as you will be avoiding refined flour and dairy. You can reduce the sugar content as they are still delicious with less sugar, or replace it with stevia granules. Raw cacao is a powerful anti-oxidant and gelatine is not only beneficial for joint, skin and hair health, but also can assist in healing a leaky gut.

1¼ tbsp powdered gelatine

3 tbsp water

1 (400 g) tin coconut cream

½ cup raw cacao powder

4 tbsp brown sugar

coconut flakes to serve

salt to taste

Mix the gelatine with the water in a small bowl and set aside for 5 minutes to allow the gelatine granules to expand and soften.

Place the coconut cream, cacao powder, sugar and salt in a saucepan over medium heat and whisk to combine. Bring to just below simmering point and remove from the heat.

Add the gelatine mixture to the warm coconut milk mixture and stir until the gelatine dissolves. Transfer to four 150 ml ramekins and place in the fridge for one hour to set.

To serve add a few coconut shavings.

# The Good Gut's Brownies for your Bacteria

Makes 16 brownies

This is another delightful gut-friendly recipe from *The Good Gut*. Here is the introduction by the authors, Erica and Justin Sonnenburg: "At some point chocolate got a bad rap, which it rightly deserves when consumed in its ultra-sweetened milk chocolate candy bar form. But more and more studies are showing that dark chocolate that contains at least 70% cocoa can be a healthy treat due to the presence of flavonoids. Chocolate also has another magic ingredient, fibre. A 25 g serving of dark chocolate contains about 3 grams of dietary fibre. In this recipe we combine chocolate and another rising star in the healthy food category, nuts, for a brownie treat that kids, adults and their microbes will love."

5 tbsp unsalted, cultured butter or ghee
100 g dark chocolate (70% cocoa)
1 cup almond meal
⅓ cup brown sugar
1 tbsp cacao nibs
2 large eggs
1 tsp vanilla extract
1 tsp ground cinnamon
1 tsp sea salt
1 tbsp orange zest

Preheat the oven to 180˚C.

Melt the butter and chocolate in a saucepot on low heat, stirring occasionally to make sure the chocolate doesn't burn.

Add the almond meal, sugar, cacao nibs, eggs, vanilla, cinnamon, salt and orange zest and whisk until all ingredients are incorporated. Pour into a 20x20 cm greased baking pan.

Bake for 30 minutes or until a toothpick inserted in the centre comes out clean.

# The Good Gut's Microbe-friendly Oatmeal Cookies

Makes 2 dozen cookies

This recipe has also been generously shared by the authors of *The Good Gut*, Justin and Erica Sonnenburg. Here is their introduction: "These cookies are a version of the standard oatmeal chocolate chip recipe but modified to better feed the microbiome. We replace the chocolate chips with cacao nibs, which are pieces of cacao beans that have been fermented and roasted. (Cacao nibs are not a source of live active cultures because the organisms don't survive the roasting process.) Their taste is nutty and is reminiscent of coffee beans. There is very little flour in these cookies; they're mostly high-fibre rolled oats."

1 tbsp wheat flour

1 tsp baking powder

¼ tsp sea salt

1 tsp ground cinnamon

2 tbsp cacao nibs, crushed

¼ cup (½ stick) unsalted, cultured butter or ghee

1 ½ cups of whole rolled oats

¼ cup macadamia oil

⅓ cup brown sugar

1 large egg

Preheat the oven to 180°C.

Line a baking sheet with parchment/baking paper.

In a small bowl, combine the flour, baking powder, salt, cinnamon and cacao nibs.

In a separate bowl, melt the butter/ghee over a saucepan with boiling water, then stir the oats and macadamia oil into the melted butter. In a separate large bowl, whisk the sugar with the egg until creamy. Add the flour mixture and the oats mixture to the egg mixture and stir until combined.

Drop approximately 1 tablespoon of dough onto a baking sheet for each cookie. Bake the cookies for 8–10 minutes, until golden brown.

# Fussy Offspring

## Gut health food for kids

### INTRODUCTION

As any parent will know, convincing children to eat the healthy meals we offer them can be extremely rough sailing. For me it is a constant learning curve as my two girls' palates develop, and their preferences radically change … sometimes from day to day!

# MANTRAS FOR HEALTHY KIDS' MEALS

In this chapter I have included some fail-safe recipes that my kids always enjoy and that satisfy my mother-heart with their nutritional content.

In order for your kids to eat well it is often a combination of simply continuing to serve ONLY healthy food choices (ONLY obviously translates to 90% of the time in reality), and depriving them of junk foods. Emotionally this can be draining, but it will pay off in a huge way. It will also ensure that you don't end up cooking two separate meals at supper. I prescribe to the 5 vegetables + 2 fruits per day philosophy (and even more veggies if you can manage it).

For good gut health kids need to have a diet rich in wholefoods that provide the fibre for good bacteria to thrive. Children tend to prefer fruit over vegetables and I allow my kids more than 2 fruits per day despite the sugar content, to increase their fibre intake. Healthy active children can certainly cope with some natural sugar, and in addition fruit provides wonderful vitamins and phytonutrients too.

Below are some of my mama-mantras when it comes to healthy eating for my kids:

1. Hunger is the best cook. This may sound extreme, but in reality feeling a bit hungry before dinner is a wonderful way to get kids to try healthy foods and eat what you have prepared. Hunger can also cause initial meltdowns, but I find that once those initial two or three bites have hit their tummy they eat quite happily.

2. Educating your kids about the difference between good and bad foods is extremely important. Use fun analogies and stories to teach them what the benefits are of eating well; 'because it's good for you' won't stick, they need clever and interesting explanations that can also provide fun dinner conversation and bonding time as a family. Once they understand why they can't live on blue cereal and fake foods such as viennas they can take responsibility for their own health when they are offered these foods elsewhere.

3. Grate, blend or mash up vegetables and hide them in the sauce. This is of course cheating in your quest to get your kids to learn to love vegetables, but if they won't touch vegetables this will at least allow you to sleep better at night.

4. Let them prepare food. It's difficult for kids to resist eating what they've cooked themselves; it's also a fabulous bargaining tool to use when you can say: 'I ate the supper you cooked for me, so you should eat mine.'

5. Grow some veggies. If they have grown it themselves, they will most probably eat it too. The additional microbe exposure from working with soil is fabulous too.

I am a firm believer that offering healthy choices throughout your children's formative years creates a 'blueprint' for them. Even if it remains a battle to get them to eat those healthy meals you have prepared, there will be a much better chance of them reverting to this healthy blueprint when they become adults and can make their own food choices.

# Monkey Business Smoothie

Serves 2–4

We are early risers, but sometimes everyone wakes up on the disorganised, slow side of the bed. On mornings like these it seems impossible to get a proper breakfast made for to my two girls, and that's when this smoothie comes to the rescue. It can even be enjoyed in a travel cup in the car en route to school. It delivers the right kind of fibre for their microbes, as well as enough protein and good fats to fuel brain and body until snack-time at school.

¼ cup peanut butter

½ cup full fat live Greek yoghurt

2 small bananas

1 tbsp honey

1 heaped tbsp cacao, maca & chia seed powder (I use Wholefood Connection's version readily available from Wellness Warehouse or selected supermarkets)

½ cup A2 milk (for a runnier consistency)

Simply add all the ingredients to your blender jug and whiz together until you have smooth mixture.

# French Toast Soldiers

French toast, also affectionately known as 'eggy-bread' in our house, is another super-fast nutritious meal I make my kids for breakfast, or to add to their lunch boxes. I usually serve it with some sliced apple or banana for added fibre and enzymes, and I recommend using true sourdough bread made from unbleached, non-GMO flour, available from most reputable bakeries. If you don't always have time to stop by a bakery, buy in bulk when you can, slice your loaves and them freeze them in batches so you can take out a few slices when needed. As mentioned in the chapter Lunchbox Love, bread (or any wheat flour foods such as pasta, etc.) should be a 'now and again' addition to your diet and when choosing these foods, be picky about the origin, processing and baking method of the flour used.

2–3 large slices sourdough bread
1 large egg, beaten
ghee
Optional toppings: ghee & Marmite/
    Bovril or raw honey/real maple
    syrup

Simply slice the bread into 'soldiers' (cutting it lengthways in about 2.5 cm strips), then dip them into the beaten egg and fry them either side until golden in a little ghee. Serve them with some maple syrup or honey drizzled over them or a thin layer of Marmite/Bovril for a savoury version.

# Breakfast on a Stick

I have noticed that anything served on a stick always goes down well in the little people's books, hence my 'egg lollies'. I endeavour to include eggs in my kid's breakfasts at least three school mornings per week, but variety remains the key in getting them to eat what is served most successfully.

choice of fruit to be skewered

4 x bamboo skewers

3 eggs, whisked well

1 tbsp ghee

½–1 tsp Marmite/Bovril (or preservative- and additive-free tomoato sauce)

¼ cup white cheddar, finely grated (optional)

Start by prepping and assembling the fruit skewers, then set them aside.

Heat the ghee in a non-stick pan over medium to high heat, then pour the whisked eggs into the pan and swirl it around so the whole base of the pan has an egg layer on it.

Turn the heat down to medium-low, and allow the egg to cook until it's almost fully solidified into an open omelette, then turn it over carefully with a spatula and allow 1 more minute of cooking time before sliding onto a plate.

Next add a thin layer of Bovril/Marmite/tomato sauce over the entire surface on one side, followed by a thin layer of grated cheddar, before rolling it up as tightly as you can without breaking the egg omelette.

Slice it into 1.5 cm thick discs/medallions and skewer it onto some bamboo skewers.

# Chocolate Granola

Makes 6 portions

My kids and I love granola, and we love chocolate, so for me this is a match made in heaven. I use 90% cocoa solids chocolate which translates into an abundance of antioxidants and very little sugar.

2 cups whole rolled oats
1 heaped tbsp coconut oil
½ tsp finely ground pink salt
1 cup sunflower seeds
3 tbsp peanut butter (make sure it
   doesn't contain hydrogenated oil),
   or you can replace the peanut butter
   with macadamia or cashew butter
1 cup coarsely desiccated coconut
50 g 90% dark chocolate

Preheat the oven to 150°C.

Use a fairly deep baking tray. Add the oats, coconut oil and salt, and then place it in the oven for 5 minutes.

After 5 minutes remove and give it a good stir to make sure that the coconut oil is evenly distributed through the oats. Return the oats to the oven for a further 15 minutes.

Remove after 15 minutes, giving it a good stir and then add the sunflower seeds and peanut butter. Stir through well, and return it to the oven for a further 10 minutes.

Remove, add the coconut and chocolate and pop back in the oven for 2 minutes until the chocolate has melted. Remove and stir to make sure all the ingredients are covered in chocolate and return the tray once more to the oven for 5 more minutes.

Lastly remove the tray from the oven and allow to cool completely before storing in an airtight glass container.

Enjoy with some tahini or full-fat live yoghurt, honey or real maple syrup.

# Banana Flour Pancakes — Serves 2–4

Kids love these and you can feel quite smug when another wheat-free meal has been served to your family. Bananas are rich in inulin, a resistant starch that travels all the way to the large intestine where it becomes food for your good bacteria.

¾ cup banana flour
2 eggs
1 tsp bicarbonate of soda (baking soda)
salt to taste
50 ml of A2 milk, water or a milk substitute like coconut/almond or rice milk
ghee or coconut oil

Simply add all the ingredients, except the ghee/coconut oil, to a mixing bowl and beat well until you have a smooth consistency.

Then scoop/pour the batter into a hot pan that has been coated with a ghee/coconut oil. The size of each pancake should more or less resemble that of an American pancake, or 'crumpet'.

Wait for small bubbles to appear on the surface before turning over, aiming for an attractive golden appearance and then serve with your choice of topping.

*Note:* Top with fresh berries/bananas, yoghurt and raw honey. For a more savoury option try streaky bacon with some real maple syrup

# *Pulse Pastas*

Serves 2–3

Every mama will know that kids adore pasta. Pulse pasta in my opinion really is the healthiest alternative as corn and rice pasta are just adding another kind of refined white flour to your children's diet (albeit gluten free). Pulse pastas are not only gluten free, but also full of gut-loving fibre and high in protein and are available in most major supermarkets or online health food stores.

I usually keep these pulse pastas vegetarian as they contain plenty of protein from the pulses they are made from. For added fibre, nutrients and enzymes I usually serve these with some veggie sticks (my kids enjoy cucumber, carrot & red peppers) on the side.

## Red Pulse Pasta

1 clove garlic
1 tbsp ghee
½ cup tomato passata sauce
½ tsp brown sugar
salt to taste
150 g pulse pasta
¼ cup pecorino cheese, finely grated (optional)

In a saucepan fry the garlic in the ghee for a minute or 2 and then add the passata, sugar and salt. Allow to simmer on low heat without a lid on for 15 minutes.

Simply cook your preferred pulse pasta according to the package instructions in some salted water, drain well and stir through the cooked tomato sauce. Serve it with a sprinkling of grated pecorino cheese for added omega 3.

## Green Pulse Pasta

150 g pulse pasta
2 heaped tbsp fresh pesto

Pesto is a great favourite in our home, especially the traditional basil pesto. I adore Pesto Princess's versions that are free from unnecessary additives and flavourings.

Simply cook your preferred pulse pasta according to the package instructions in some salted water, drain well and stir through your choice of fresh pesto.

## Nutritional Yeast & Ghee Pasta

This is such an easy recipe I almost feel embarrassed to share it, but it has great nutrition and is packed with fibre. Nutritional yeast is de-activated yeast and a powerhouse of nutrients, and as an added bonus it's delicious.

1–2 tbsp ghee

2 heaped tbsp nutritional yeast
   flakes

150 g pulse pasta

Simply add 1 tablespoon (or 2) of ghee, as well as 2 tablespoons of nutritional yeast flakes (or 1 teaspoon Marmite/Bovril) to the pasta once it has been drained of all excess water and is still piping hot. Stir through well and serve.

# 'Invisible Veggie' Bolognaise/Lasagne

Serves 8

Sneak some vegetables into your little folks with this recipe. Most of the grated veggies 'disappear' in the sauce, and to really make this a fabulously healthy meal, fool them with some pulse pasta spaghetti now available at most supermarkets. This sauce can also be used as the tomato/meat sauce in lasagne, and despite running the risk of sounding like a broken record, look out for lasagne sheets made from pulses too.

1 tbsp ghee or coconut oil

2 yellow/brown onions, grated

200–300 g ground beef

2 tsp ground coriander

salt to taste

4 carrots, grated

4 courgettes (zucchini), grated

150 g mushrooms (white or brown) stems removed and grated

500 ml (2 cups) tomato passata

2 tsp sweet basil

1 tsp brown sugar

1 tbsp chicken or vegetable stock powder

pecorino cheese, finely grated for garnish (optional)

Start by sautéing the onions until they are golden and sweet, and then add the ground beef, coriander and salt, and sauté for a further 5 minutes, separating the beef into a crumbly consistency with a fork while it cooks over low heat.

Then add the grated carrots, courgettes and mushrooms and sauté, stirring frequently for another 10 minutes. Add the passata, sweet basil, sugar and stock powder. Stir through well and turn the heat down to low. Put the lid on the pot, allowing it to simmer for 30 minutes.

When it has simmered for 30 minutes serve it over some pulse pasta, or even 'zoodles' (spiralised courgette (zucchini) noodles). Garnish with pecorino cheese if you wish.

Note: If you are using this meat sauce for a lasagne, see page 137 for my gut-friendly white sauce recipe.

# Nachos Grande

Serves 4–6

Once you've made this for your family and watched how they've gobbled it all up without your usual gentle encouragement (translation: begging/pleading/threatening), you may as well sew yourself a cape with a rather large S and M embroidered on it, because I guarantee you will feel like Super Mom since you have just successfully fed your little tribe some super gut-friendly goodness.

300 g ground beef

salt to taste

½ cup tomato passata

½ tsp brown sugar

1 heaped tbsp ground cumin

1 tsp ground coriander

corn chips

3 spring onions, finely sliced

½ cup grated mozzarella

1 cup sweetcorn, thawed from frozen and all excess liquid drained

½ cup live Greek yoghurt

Holy Guacamole (see page 115)

Season the mince with salt, and then brown, using a fork to loosen it into a crumbly consistency.

Add the passata, a sprinkle of sugar to regulate the acidity in the passata, as well as the cumin and coriander. Stir through and allow to simmer for approximately 20 minutes on low heat without a lid.

Next spread the corn chips out in a large and fairly deep baking tray.

Once the beef sauce is ready, cover the nachos fairly evenly with meat sauce (it's fine if there are gaps here and there). Then sprinkle over the spring onions, cheese and sweetcorn.

Pop it under the grill for 5 minutes to allow the cheese to melt. Add blobs of guacamole and Greek yoghurt over the cheese/meat/corn layer and serve immediately.

# Shepherd's Pie for Fussy Offspring

Serves 4

4 tbsp ghee or coconut oil

3 yellow/brown onions, finely chopped (or even minced/grated for fussy eaters)

300 g ground beef

1 tsp sweet paprika

1 tbsp ground coriander

salt and pepper to taste

6 courgettes (zucchini), grated

3 carrots, grated

1 heaped tbsp chickpea flour (optional)

2 tbsp nutritional yeast flakes (optional)

4–6 jewel (orange flesh) sweet potatoes

In a deep ovenproof pot or saucepan, sauté the onions in 1 tbsp of ghee until they are golden and sweet, then add the ground beef, paprika, coriander and salt. Sauté for a further 5 minutes, separating the beef into a crumbly consistency with a fork while it cooks over low heat.

Now add the grated carrot and courgettes and sauté for another 10 minutes, stirring occasionally.

Sprinkle over the chickpea flour and nutritional yeast and stir through well, adding a little more salt if desired. Pop the lid on the pot and allow the beef and vegetables to cook over low heat for 10 minutes.

*Mash:* Peel and halve the sweet potatoes, and then boil them in water until they are tender. Drain most of the cooking water, only retaining approximately ¼ cup, and then add the rest of the ghee and mash until you have a silky smooth consistency.

Lastly take the ground beef filling off the heat and spread out the sweet potato mash over it evenly. Pop it under the grill for 5–10 minutes to produce a satisfying crispy top, and then serve.

# Munchies for your Microbes

## Gut-healthy snacks

### INTRODUCTION

These simple snack recipes are full of fibre and quality
nutrients, as well as being gluten free.

# Popcorn

## *The Good Gut's* Japanese Popcorn

Serves 2

This is such a delicious and healthy homemade treat, I think I am quite addicted to it. Here is the introduction to it from Justin and Erica Sonnenburg, authors of *The Good Gut*:

"Even if you don't have a microbiome with seaweed-degrading porphyranases there are still many reasons to eat sea vegetables. They are loaded with an assortment of minerals and have a complex seafood flavour. Sprinkle nori on fibre-loaded popcorn (which is a whole grain) to make a healthy treat for you and your microbiota."

1 tsp coconut oil
⅓ cup popcorn kernels
2 tbsp sesame oil
2 nori sheets, crushed
1 tsp wasabi powder or cayenne pepper
(optional)
½ tsp sea salt

In a large pot heat 1 tbsp of coconut oil on high heat, add the popcorn kernels and cover.

Once the kernels begin to pop, shake the pan vigorously. When the popping subsides, remove the pot from the heat immediately to avoid burning the popcorn. Transfer the popcorn to a rimmed baking sheet.

Drizzle the sesame oil over the popcorn and sprinkle it with the crushed nori and wasabi powder or cayenne (if using) for some heat and finely ground sea salt. Toss well, and serve.

# Brewer's Yeast Popcorn

Brewer's yeast is in my opinion an affordable super food supplement. Buy a brand that sells deactivated brewer's yeast in powder form. It has been grown and used as a nutritional supplement for years. Brewer's yeast is a rich source of minerals – particularly selenium, protein, B-complex vitamins and chromium, an essential trace mineral that helps the body maintain normal blood sugar levels. In addition it has a delicious taste. I make this for me and the girls as a healthy snack.

1 tbsp coconut oil
⅓ cup popcorn kernels
1 tbsp powdered brewer's yeast
1 heaped tbsp ghee
½ tsp sea salt

In a large pot heat 1 tablespoon of coconut oil on high heat, add the popcorn kernels and cover.

Once the kernels begin to pop, shake the pan vigorously. When the popping subsides, remove the pot from the heat immediately to avoid burning the popcorn. Transfer the popcorn to a rimmed baking sheet.

Heat the ghee and drizzle it over the popcorn, then sprinkle with salt and brewer's yeast and toss well before enjoying.

# The Good Gut's Filled Dates

Serves 2

Here is another lovely snack recipe from the authors of *The Good Gut*. Justin and Erica Sonnenburg share their thoughts about it here: "Medjools are often called the king of dates. They can be expensive but they have such a satisfying taste that just a couple can keep your appetite appeased until dinner. Serve with an optional sprinkle of cinnamon."

8 medjool dates
3 tbsp cultured (live) cream cheese
8 walnut halves
ground cinnamon (optional)

Slit open one side of the date to remove the pit. Stuff a generous teaspoon of cream cheese and a walnut half into each date. Serve with an optional sprinkle of cinnamon.

# The Good Gut's Cashews for your Commensals

Makes 4 cups

I am delighted to share yet another healthy and delicious snack recipe from *The Good Gut*, authored by Justin and Erica Sonnenburg. They say: "Turmeric is medicinal for its anti-inflammatory properties. We try to incorporate this spice into dishes whenever we can. Paired with cashews, this Middle Eastern-style snack is both tasty and filled with microbiota-accessible carbohydrates."

1 tbsp macadamia oil

4 cups raw cashews

1 tsp sea salt

1 tbsp ground turmeric

Heat the oil in a medium skillet over medium-high heat. Add the cashews and sprinkle with sea salt. Roast the cashews while stirring frequently, about 5 minutes, then remove from the heat and toss in the turmeric. Cool and store in a jar with a tight-fitting lid.

# Yoghurt Parfait

As far as I am concerned the combination of yoghurt and honey is just lovely. Adding some crunch, good fats and fibre with nuts, berries, etc. will not only will carry you through to the next meal, but also nourish your body and promote better gut health. You can get creative and add different fruits, nuts and other fibre-filled natural toppings for variety.

½ cup live full fat Greek yoghurt

1 tbsp of tahini or macadamia butter

¼ cup berries

handful of air-roasted nuts (walnuts or
   cashews work well)

1 tsp raw untreated honey

dried fruit such as naartjie, mango or
   pineapple (optional)

Simply add the yoghurt to a bowl or glass and top with fresh berries, tahini/butter, nuts, dried fruit and raw honey.

# Chocolate Bombs

These serve as wonderful fuel for when you don't have enough time for a proper meal or just before a workout. As treats go, these are pretty gut and kid friendly too.

½ cup air-roasted cashews

⅓ cup coconut oil

⅓ cup pitted dates

⅔ cup almond butter

½ cup desiccated coconut

½ cup raw cacao powder

salt to taste

Add the cashews to your blender jug and pulse until you have a crumbly consistency, then scoop out half of the cashew crumbs and set aside on a plate for your balls to be rolled in later.

Now add all the other ingredients (along with half of the cashews) into your blender jug and pulse until you have a fairly smooth, sticky consistency. Remove the mixture one tablespoon at a time and roll with clean hands into small balls. Lastly, roll them in the remaining cashew crumbs before transferring them to a flat and wide container that can be sealed with a lid or cling film. Store them to the fridge for up to 2 weeks.

# *Low-carb Granola Bars* Makes 8–10 bars

I love granola bars as a breakfast on the run. They are also great lunch box additions and crammed full of protein and gut-healthy fibre. Oats are one of the yummiest gut-healthy foods out there. Not only are these bars delicious, but they also boost some beneficial bacteria in the gastrointestinal tract which can provide serious relief in cases of irritable bowel disease and constipation.

¼ cup real maple syrup or raw untreated honey

¼ cup smooth peanut butter or cashew butter

1 cup air-roasted unsalted almonds or cashews, coarsely chopped

1 cup whole rolled oats

½ cup raw sunflower seeds

2 tbsp psyllium husks

3 tbsp chickpea flour

salt to taste

Add all the ingredients to a large mixing bowl and then stir it through well.

Once thoroughly mixed, transfer to a fairly deep baking tin (square or rectangular in shape) lined with parchment/ baking paper. Press down firmly until uniformly flattened – I use something flat, like a drinking glass, to press down and really pack the bars, which helps them hold together better.

Cover with parchment or plastic wrap, and let firm up in fridge or freezer for 15–20 minutes. Preheat the oven to 150°C while you wait.

Bake for 15 minutes. Allow to cool completly before slicing into 10 even bars (or 9 squares). Store them in an airtight container for up to a week.

# About the author

Marlien Wright is also the author of the cookbook *The Yoga Kitchen: 100 Easy Superfood Recipes*. She is a mom, yogi, nutrition coach and food writer. She enjoys eating real food and creating healthy #foodporn. She believes that being healthy is sexy, insists on living authentically and honestly, and diving in at the deep end. Marlien and her girls live in Hout Bay, Cape Town. To stay in touch with Marlien's food journey, her upcoming retreats and workshops, head on over to www.yogakitchen.co.za

# Index